THE CHANGI CAMERA

CAMERA

A UNIQUE RECORD OF CHANGI AND THE THAI-BURMA RAILWAY

TIM BOWDEN

hachette
AUSTRALIA

hachette
AUSTRALIA

Published in Australia and New Zealand in 2012
by Hachette Australia
(an imprint of Hachette Australia Pty Limited)
Level 17, 207 Kent Street, Sydney NSW 2000
www.hachette.com.au

Originally published in 1984 as *Changi Photographer: George Aspinall's record of captivity*

This revised and expanded version published in 2012

National Library of Australia
Cataloguing-in-Publication data

Bowden, Tim, 1937-
The Changi camera : George Aspinall's photographs and memories / Tim Bowden.

9780733629624 (hbk.)

    Aspinall, George, 1923–1991.
    Burma–Siam Railroad.
    Soldiers – Australia – Biography.
    Prisoners of war – Singapore – Changi – Biography
    World War, 1939–1945 – Photography.
    Changi POW Camp (Changi, Singapore)

940.540092

Jacket design by Christabella Designs
Author photo (p. vi) courtesy Tim Bowden
All other photos taken by George Aspinall
Text design by Bookhouse, Sydney
Typeset in 12.75/17 pt Garamond Premier Pro
Printed and bound by Everbest Printing Co Ltd

Hachette Australia's policy is to use papers that are natural, renewable and recyclable products
and made from wood grown in sustainable forests. The logging and manufacturing processes
are expected to conform to the environmental regulations of the country of origin.

TO MY FRIEND HANK NELSON,
for his invaluable guidance and scholarship

CONTENTS

Tim Bowden, ABC producer, edits interviews with former Australian prisoners of war in 1982, for the sixteen-part radio documentary series, *Prisoners of War – Australians under Nippon*.

AUTHOR'S NOTE

IN THE EARLY 1980S, WHEN HISTORIAN HANK NELSON AND I BEGAN INTERVIEWING AUSTRALIANS who had been prisoners of war of the Japanese in South-east Asia during World War II for a radio documentary series for the ABC, there had been very little public awareness of their experiences. Hank felt that enough time had gone by for them to reflect on and talk frankly about their experiences in South-east Asia, and that turned out to be so. Military historians tend to concentrate on campaigns and battles and not the experiences of captured soldiers – although POW casualties in South-east Asia had been heavy. Because they were captured alive (rather than committing suicide as the Japanese Bushido code ordained) they were not only treated with derision by their captors, but also forced to work as slave labour for huge projects including the Thai–Burma Railway.

The former prisoners of war were themselves partly responsible for their lack of recognition, because of a feeling of collective guilt that they had become prisoners of war – although many had fought extremely gallant but short battles before their enforced surrender on Singapore island. Yet it is hard to think of active service life providing any greater hardship than they endured as POWs: not knowing whether they would die of dysentery, untreated tropical diseases, starvation, or the random act of a brutal guard. The sixteen-part radio documentary series *Prisoners Of War – Australians Under Nippon*, first broadcast in 1984, can partly be credited with raising awareness of what these men and women endured. Many spoke frankly on tape about experiences they had not even told their own families.

Those broadcasts also triggered a new debate on the Australian POW experiences in South-east Asia. More books and memoirs were written and more attention paid to what the 8th Division men had been through. It would have been unthinkable, before this surge of interest, for an Australian prime minister to celebrate Anzac Day by travelling to Hellfire Pass on the old Thai–Burma Railway. John Howard was there in 1998.

One of my interviewees was George Aspinall. After our two-hour talk, I asked him how many of his photographs had survived. He pulled open a desk drawer, revealing a jumbled mass of prints and negatives as he rummaged about. 'Oh, I think about eighty or a hundred,' he said. George then agreed to co-operate in a book, and so began many more interviewing sessions where I homed in on the detail that his remarkable memory was able to provide. The original *Changi Photographer: George Aspinall's Record of Captivity* was published by ABC Books in 1984, and subsequently reprinted many times.

George's passionate hobby post war was filming steam trains, and he also filmed former prisoners of war visiting the remains of the Thai–Burma Railway for the New South Wales Ex-Prisoners of War Association. He was a very private and humble man, and was delighted with the book's success. Like many of his generation he was a lifelong smoker and, sadly, died on 28 October 1991. He was 68 years old.

When, in the new millennium, Matthew Kelly, Non-Fiction Publisher at Hachette Australia approached me with the idea of a new edition, I was absolutely delighted that George's remarkable story was to be published again. He would have been, too.

Tim Bowden

George Aspinall, aged eighteen

INTRODUCTION

THE SHADOWY AND EVOCATIVE SERIES OF PHOTOGRAPHS TAKEN BY GEORGE ASPINALL IN Singapore, Malaya and Thailand in 1942 and 1943 is the most comprehensive photographic record obtained by an Australian prisoner of war of the Japanese. The photographs survived not only because of the skill and daring displayed by the teenage boy who took them, but because Aspinall knew that, unless he processed his films, they would be destroyed by the hothouse humidity of the tropical climate. Indeed the ingenuity and tenacity he displayed to obtain film stock and chemicals to process his negatives form some of the most intriguing elements of the story of the Aspinall photographs.

Private George Aspinall joined the AIF at the tender age of seventeen (making use of his cousin's birth certificate) and was sent overseas with the 2/30th Battalion to Singapore in 1941. He was then eighteen. He celebrated his nineteenth birthday as a prisoner of war of the Imperial Japanese Army on Singapore's Changi Peninsula on 18 October 1942. By then he was already taking secret photographs with the folding Kodak 2 camera given to him by his uncle in Wagga Wagga.

Not long after the fall of Singapore in February 1942, George Aspinall was working on the docks in a slave labour gang, loading war loot on ships bound for Japan. In one of the warehouses, known as godowns, he came across a stock of X-ray photographic material, including some large sheets of X-ray negatives and bottles of developer; and by opening other bottles and sniffing until he thought he recognised the distinctive odour he also found hypo (fixer). By trial and error, he learned to process his negatives, which were then stored in a Town Talk tobacco tin.

He carried his camera in a secret pocket in a canvas kidney belt, and began to capture daily details of prisoner-of-war life on film. It is significant that George was not, at that stage, setting out to make a documentary record, or trying to highlight Japanese atrocities. He was taking pictures with the idea of keeping them to show his mother and relatives, continuing the general photographs he had been taking since he arrived in Malaya. He worked in the tradition of a family photographer producing an album of significant snaps. The photographs became his visual diary of captivity, even though he risked his life every time he took a picture. The method was laborious. He would decide, usually the day before, what picture he wanted to take. During the darkness of the night he would load one piece of X-ray negative into the body of his camera. There was only once chance each day, and sometimes groups of his friends would shield him as he used his camera.

His most remarkable achievement, though, was to smuggle his camera, negatives, and developing chemicals up to the infamous Thai–Burma death railway, and document the appalling privations suffered by F Force in the Three Pagodas Pass area of the railway. His photographs of the so-called 'fit' workers, ribs protruding, stomachs and legs distended and swollen with water beriberi, reproduced the horror of those times more vividly than any written diary. He photographed the dreadful Cholera Camp at Shimo Sonkurai No 1 Camp, and the ghastly tropical ulcers that ate into the legs of his companions – sometimes leading to amputation, often without anaesthetic. At night he would go down to a nearby creek, and with a piece of old groundsheet over his head to shield the exposed film from the moon or starlight, he would laboriously process each X-ray negative.

Unfortunately some very thorough searches by the Japanese military police, the feared *Kempeitai*, forced George Aspinall to break up his beloved Kodak 2 camera and throw the pieces down a deep well in Thailand during the return from the Thai–Burma Railway in 1943. But he kept the processed negatives and they were eventually buried in a canister down a toilet bore-hole in the grounds of Changi Gaol, to be recovered after the war.

Not all George Aspinall's photographs have survived. Some were ruined by the damp and humidity on the Thai–Burma Railway, and after they were buried down the bore-hole. Other photographs were lost, after having been sent to the Rabaul war crimes trials, which began in 1946, as pictorial evidence of Japanese brutality.

Some 22,000 Australians went into Japanese prisoner-of-war camps in 1942 and about 14,000 survived their three-and-a-half years of captivity. George Aspinall's collection of photographs constitute an extraordinary record of those desperate years, when British, Australian, Dutch and American troops were being driven beyond endurance as slave labour of the Imperial Japanese Army.

PART I
The POW Experience

TIM BOWDEN

THE CHANGI EXPERIENCE

THE NAME 'CHANGI' HAS A JARRING, JANGLING, EVEN SINISTER RESONANCE AND RIGHTLY OR wrongly became a byword for all the indignities and atrocities committed by the Japanese towards the Allied servicemen and women captured by them in 1942 following the battle for Malaya.

It is difficult now to comprehend the enormity of the shock in Australia and Britain, when Singapore – that supposedly impregnable fortress – fell so quickly to the invading forces of the Imperial Japanese Army carving their remorseless way down the Malay Peninsula. The surrender on 15 February 1942 signalled the end of not only the old colonial empires in South-East Asia, but eventually India too.

The most bewildered were the 15,000 Australians and 35,000 British troops on Singapore Island facing up to an uncertain future as prisoners of war of the Japanese. They had no idea of what this might entail, as they had never envisaged it happening. The cultural divide was absolute. The Japanese Bushido code demanded that a soldier should either die in battle or commit suicide if captured. The

3

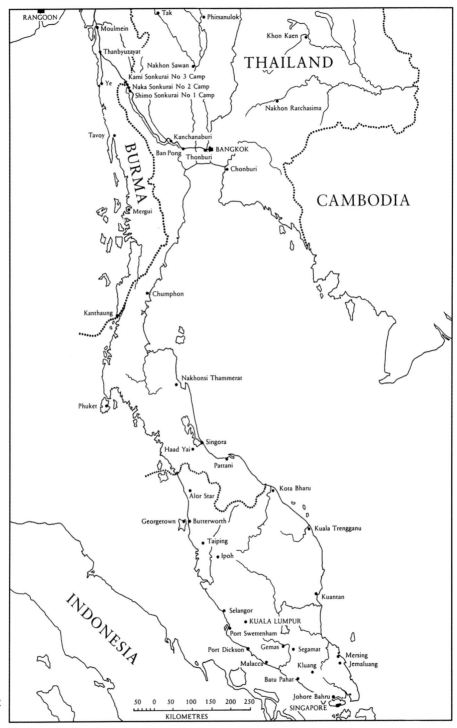

South-east
Asia

Japanese soldiers could not understand why so many Allied troops were prepared to become POWs, and were contemptuous of them as being men without honour. The Australians and British looked at it differently, and looked forward to getting home, eventually.

Faced with 50,000 captured Allied troops who were not going anywhere, the Japanese made a very smart decision. Not wanting to waste their fighting troops on looking after prisoners of war, they decided to leave the British and Australian military command structures intact, so that they could effectively continue to look after themselves. Eventually the former British barracks, badly damaged by bombing, where the POWs assembled on the Changi Peninsula on the south-east tip of Singapore island were surrounded with a perimeter of barbed wire (ordered to be constructed by the prisoners themselves), with just enough Japanese guards to ensure security.

The Allied soldiers had absolutely no idea how they would be treated by their Japanese captors, and they were right to be apprehensive.

Perhaps the most telling example of the extremes of POW treatment is what happened to Private Keith Botterill of the 2/29th Battalion as a prisoner of war. Immediately after the surrender and after only a few days in Changi, he was sent to work on the small island of Pulau Bukum, a petrol storage depot just south of Singapore. The work was hard, but there were no bashings, and there was plenty of food. At night a rather fussy and uncharacteristically caring Japanese guard used to come around to where the Australian POW workers were sleeping and tuck their mosquito nets in so that they would be protected from malaria.

Eventually Keith and his mate got bored. Botterill:

Me mate says, 'This is no good, Keith, working on a Saturday, let's get back to Changi.' I said, 'I'll be in that. Blow this working Saturday. Blow working at all.' We just said, 'Oh we're crook.' The doctor repeated, 'These men are sick,' so the Japanese put about ten of us on a little boat, and took us to Singapore about ten miles away, unloaded us, and put us on a truck.

We were about half a mile down the street when there's a flaming head sticking on a post. A fresh head, and a warning – THIS WILL HAPPEN TO YOU IF YOU TRY TO ESCAPE OR BETRAY US OR CAUSE ANY MISCHIEF.

This is lovely! Next corner, another head – and a head on every corner. We get back to Changi. There's a draft going away tomorrow, another working party. So I got on B Force. That's how I came to get to Borneo.

It was not a felicitous choice. Botterill had booked his passage to Sandakan, site of the worst atrocity committed against Allied POWs by the Japanese in the whole Pacific War, when in late 1944 and early 1945 they sent 2,000 Australians and 500 British troops into the jungle and mountains of Borneo on the infamous death marches. Only six survived, and Botterill was one of them.

The main Allied POW camp at Changi was no holiday camp, and rations were always tight, but those lucky enough to stay in it for the duration rarely saw a Japanese soldier, were under an Allied administration, and had access to the best medical services available to any prisoner-of-war camp in South-East Asia.

In comparison with the horrors of forced labour on the Thai–Burma Railway, where one in three Australian and British soldiers died, Changi was 'like heaven' as Fred Stringer, a member of the Changi Concert Party, put it.

The Australians of the 8th Division did not expect to become prisoners of war. In their training, prejudice had replaced military intelligence. The Japanese soldiers were portrayed by instructors as near-sighted dwarfs, their equipment sub-standard and their fighting abilities poor. Sergeant Stan Arneil remembers being told that the Japanese troops were:

> . . . all half blind of course. And there was this brigade major who lectured us how the Japanese set off crackers at night time, and we wouldn't be frightened of that. We said, no, we wouldn't be frightened of crackers.

Cliff Moss was comforted by stories that 'their rifles were no good. You could squeeze the bullets out like blackheads.' That was if the myopic Japanese were ever able to hit anyone.

This nonsense was quickly dispelled after the Japanese invaded northern Malaya on 8 December 1941. General Arthur Percival, the British commander, had 70,000 front-line troops at his disposal. They comprised 38 infantry battalions – 13 British, six Australian, 17 Indian, and two Malayan – and three machine-gun battalions. They faced (as it turned out) an invasion force, commanded by General Tomoyuki Yamashita, of 30,000 well-trained, well-equipped jungle-savvy Japanese troops.

The Allies' obsolete aircraft were soon shot out of the skies, and the fearless Japanese soldiers – for whom death in combat was a divine honour sanctioned by their emperor – streamed south on bicycles or any transport they could appropriate, through the Malayan defences with astonishing efficiency. They were directed by their tough and resourceful commander, General Yamashita. The Indian troops opposing them, well aware of moves for independence against the British Raj at home, were ambivalent about fighting for their colonial masters in Malaya, and although some fought bravely, other units just melted away. Realising this, the Japanese began signing the Indian troops over to their cause, and many obliged, eventually to become the gaolers of their former rulers.

The toughest of the Japanese invading forces were the Imperial Japanese Guard, six-footers most of them, and fresh from China where they had a policy of not taking prisoners. Their eyesight was impeccable, and their marksmanship irreproachable.

The Japanese advancing down the Malay Peninsula did not clash with the Australians before the middle of January. By then the Japanese were cocky and confident and there were plenty of them. The cyclists, their rifles slung on their backs, rode into an ambush set for them by the 2/30th Battalion at Gemas. To the east, near Muar, the 2/29th Battalion and supporting gunners were soon in action. They ambushed and knocked out eight tanks, but were trapped against advancing forces with their backs to the Parit Sulong River.

Brief victories had been won by the Australians at Gemas, Muar and at Mersing in the west. But these were positive moments in long days of preparing positions and retreating again.

At Parit Sulong, the wounded had to be left behind. But the Japanese, and particularly the Japanese Imperial Guard, did not respect the Geneva Convention on wounded combatants, even if

Keppel Harbour on the morning after Singapore fell, 16 February 1942. George Aspinall:
I went walkabout on the morning after the surrender, thinking I might be able to find a boat to escape. The building in the background is the Singapore Post Office and, behind it, smoke from burning oil storage tanks at Bukit Timah is billowing up into the sky.

they had ever heard of it. Lieutenant Ben Hackney of the 2/19th Battalion was the sole survivor of a massacre:

> Try and imagine a gorilla gone berserk, and that sums up the treatment of the Japanese. They had no care whatsoever for anything. Bayonets, rifle butts, anything used anywhere.

Hackney had been wounded and captured at Parit Sulong, and was among 110 Australians and 50 Indians who were bashed and bayoneted. Hackney, pretending to be dead even as his boots were dragged off him, was left while those bodies judged to be still alive were piled in a heap, machine-gunned, doused with petrol and burnt.

Other captured Australian and British troops were treated more reasonably by front-line soldiers, despite the disgrace – in Japanese eyes – of allowing themselves to be captured alive. Most Japanese soldiers had never seen a European closely before, and curiosity came before the Imperial edicts forbidding surrender.

By 31 January, barely six weeks after the Japanese had landed, the last retreating Allied forces had crossed the causeway from Johor Bahru to Singapore Island, blown a hole in it, and prepared to defend Britain's notional 'impregnable fortress'.

Two weeks later, on 15 February, after massive bombing and civilian casualties (accompanied by fierce fighting by the besieged Allied forces), with Singapore's water supply cut off from Malaya, and a clearly hopeless situation with no possibility of reinforcements, the British commander General Arthur Percival announced an unconditional surrender.

The victorious Japanese faced some formidable logistical problems. The city of Singapore had been badly damaged in the bombing. To add to that, there were now nearly 15,000 Australians and 35,000 British troops who were prisoners of war. What to do with them?

The Australian troops were aghast at the sudden surrender, wondering how it could have happened so quickly with all the forces the Allies had at their disposal, and also angry at their sudden switch from active fighting soldiers to prisoners of war. They had thought about their chances of being killed or wounded, but few had considered being taken prisoner. They had clung to the hope of a last stand, or holding the enemy at bay for a long siege as their AIF forebears had done at Gallipoli and Tobruk.

Captain Ray Steele had been with the artillery at Muar:

> We were absolutely flabbergasted – all of us. I can remember the reactions from the various fellows: some of them just swore, some of them threw things about, some of them were just silent and shocked. We just didn't want it. We felt that we were capable of fighting on.

During the Malayan and Singapore campaigns, the Australians had lost 2,178 killed or missing and presumed dead. It had been one of the hardest campaigns fought by the AIF in World War II. Historian Hank Nelson commented: 'Many of the ex-servicemen of Malaya and Singapore regret that they have been received in Australia almost exclusively as ex-prisoners; their experiences after surrender have subsumed their identity as ex-soldiers.'

That was to come later. The Australians had yet to experience their first personal contacts with their captors, and they already knew that Japanese behaviour could vary greatly. They were right to be apprehensive, but there was curiosity on both sides.

Sergeant Jack Sloane:

> It wasn't until the next day [after the surrender] that we actually saw our first Japanese. What impressed me was that we were looked on as curios, and we were somewhat interested

in what they looked like. They seemed like ruffians. But the front-line Japanese appeared to me to be a fellow who realised that, like himself, we were just doing a job.

Some Japanese moved among the dispirited men looking for spoils. Tom Morris lost a cheap watch he had bought recently for 15 shillings. 'The little Jap already had about half a dozen on his wrist.'

Bowing to the Japanese did not come easily to Australians. On Sumatra, where there were also many Australian soldiers, Frank Robinson had his first lesson in cultural compromise:

> We were treated reasonably well by the Japanese for a start, except for the fact that we had to bow to the Japanese when we met them. That was a little bit below our dignity. We didn't like the idea of bowing to a Jap, and much to our sorrow many of us were bashed about. We decided in the finish that we'd better forget our dignity and bow to them. We realised later that to bow, and they'd bow back, was to salute them. It was just their way of life.

Two days after the surrender, the Japanese occupation command had decided to march nearly all the Allied prisoners from the city centre to the Changi Peninsula on the south-east tip of Singapore Island. Seemingly endless columns of men marched all day to get there. Don Moore marched on his twenty-second birthday:

> You could see a mass of our fellows marching forward, and when you came up a long hill you would see this long line of humanity at the back of you. There seemed to be thousands

and thousands and thousands of us. It made us puzzled. Why couldn't we have done something?

Eighteen-year-old George Aspinall was one of them, with his precious folding Kodak 2 camera in his haversack, given to him by his uncle in Wagga Wagga as a going-away present after he enlisted at the age of seventeen, using his cousin's birth certificate to get in.

Not knowing what awaited them, the soldiers carried as much as they could: tinned food, extra clothing, even bedding. But as

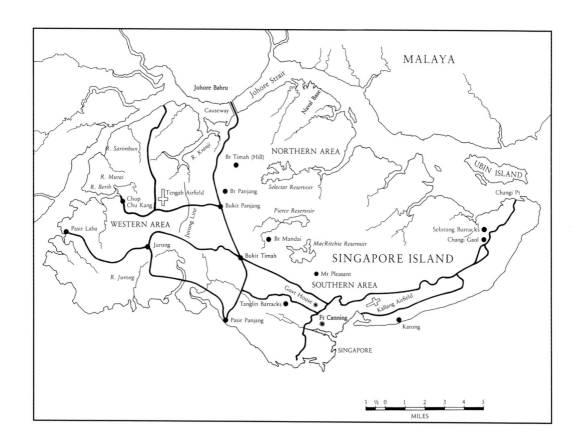

Singapore Island

the long, hot day wore on they started chucking most of it away. Aspinall noticed Japanese film crews and photographers at work capturing the long column of dejected men as they trudged along. He noticed lots of Japanese flags and thought they must have been distributed for propaganda purposes.

Singapore Chinese, living in houses along the way, risked bashings and punishment to get drinks and food to as many men as they could. But others, probably Malays, jeered at the defeated soldiers, adding to their despair. Don Moore:

> Darkness started to descend. The kampongs, the villages, were a bit more spaced. And when we were feeling a little low, the piper started up. Then it was really good. We knew he must have been as exhausted and depressed as what we were, and yet up he sounded.

Jimmy Oliver was the piper, and he was later to carry his bagpipes into the work camps.

The march had been about 29 kilometres, not a problem for fit troops, but the men were exhausted by the fighting and hungry, and morale was understandably low. The Australians had been directed to the bomb-damaged Selarang Barracks, a former top British army establishment. It was a miserable place for the arrivals, who just lay down on the concrete or the ground. Gunner Frank Christie wrote in his diary, 'All rooted, slept where we could'.

At first glance the Changi Peninsula was a most attractive place, with rolling lush hills, and views of the sea with some available beaches

– one of which was later used by Captain (later Sir Adrian) Curlewis for lifesaving instruction classes for interested Australian POWs.

The first concern was food. At first the Australians ate what they had managed to carry in, which wasn't much. Don Moore:

> We went on to some very tight rations. There was just one biscuit with bully beef pasted over it for the midday meal. In the evening, there was another meagre ration, some tinned vegetables smeared over a biscuit. Things were a little tough. We were asking, 'Can't the cooks use a little bit of imagination? Can't we get some more stuff?' 'Well, look,' said the major, 'we've got quite a few bags of rice here. It has been coming here for the past few weeks. Would you eat that?' 'Oh Jesus! What do you think you are coming at? Of course, yes, we'll eat the damned stuff!'

There was indeed rice, but as 'Snow' Peat succinctly put it, 'No bugger knew how to cook it. We weren't used to the boong type of cooking with kwalies and things like that.' The only time the army cooks had ever used rice was in rice puddings. The rice they were getting was sub-standard anyway, un-husked and weevil-infested. It took a while for the cooks to work out how to separate the grains and keep it fluffy.

There had to be a change in attitude by the army. Normally cooks were well down the pecking order, but nutrition became the primary concern underpinning all health and welfare. Dr Rowley Richards recalled how the men in the kitchen and hygiene squads had to be recruited from the most able men in the camp. War artist Murray

Griffin said it took a while, but soon the cooks 'could make rice sit up and beg. It was coloured bright green and orange, pink red and just plain white. But it was all rice, and some men could not take it.'

At first it was just boiled, watery rice – an excess of fluid and little solids. Body weight started to fall away, and men found they blacked out when they stood up. Constipation became endemic. Don Moore:

> Every POW gets hung up on bowels. Our stomach had the impact of sudden starvation placed on it, and it was painful. Some fellows went fourteen days without having a motion. When you did have a motion, the pain and the strain of it was something you won't forget.

That quickly turned to universal dysentery, and in the case of the unfortunate Jim Richardson, a life-long affliction. 'Your backside looked like the tail light on a vehicle, it just burnt your tail off. I tell you I just kept running . . .' Jim was an extreme case, with dysentery keeping him on the move not only in Changi, but up on the Thai–Burma Railway and even after the war when he returned to civilian life. Only in the early 1980s did he discover that eating raw cloves of garlic fixed him up, and thirty-odd years of uninterrupted squitters were finally banished.

Army engineers got busy and repaired the damaged infrastructure of Selarang Barracks, so that the electricity and plumbing worked again. Geoff 'Ocka' O'Connor described it as 'a resort'. Men could take a shower and read or play cards by electric light in the evening. O'Connor later told me, 'We didn't see the Japs at all. Even though we weren't eating well, we had peace of mind.' Later to be sent to the Thai–Burma Railway as part of the slave labour work gangs, O'Connor recalled his time in Changi with great affection. 'Had I been able to, I'd never have left the place. It would have done me.'

Sanitation – much needed because of all the dysentery – was organised by the engineers who drilled bore-holes with a big auger, turned by men with a crossbar. These latrines became great sources of gossip. An enduring theme was that they would all be rescued by an Allied invasion army by Christmas. These 'bore-hole rumours' of imminent rescue endured for the next three-and-a-half years. The most believed furphies were often gleaned from prisoners on working parties from 'a well-dressed Chinaman speaking perfect English.'

The belief in an early deliverance was so well entrenched that the authorities found it difficult to convince troops of the necessity of setting aside emergency medical and food supplies. That incarceration might stretch into years was simply not believed at the start of captivity.

The biggest challenge for the Australian military authorities on the Changi Peninsula was how to keep 15,000 of their troops occupied. One early concern was the libido of these still fit men, even on reduced rice rations. Military discipline was emphasised by parades, although marching about for the apparent pleasure of high-ranking visiting Japanese officers was understandably unpopular. Soon the Japanese would begin creaming off the supply of cheap labour from Changi to various work parties around Singapore and eventually far beyond, but it became apparent in those early days that sex was indeed rearing its multi-faceted head. Warrant Officer Eric Bailey:

Sleeping quarters, Selarang Barracks
We slept on makeshift beds called charpoys, made from four posts with a mattress woven from coconut-husk rope. Our bedding and washing were hung up to dry overhead. We still had plenty of clothes in those days!

Although sex wasn't talked about in later years, obviously in the early stages it was very much thought of because it was cut off very suddenly. The boys were still very healthy. One of my jobs was to go round at night because certain couples were known to be going to particular spots and indulging in homosexuality. I was supposed to break it up, tell them to get back to their separate bunks. It seemed to be getting so bad that our officers went to the Japanese and asked them would they give the soldiers some long trenches to dig. And so they dug those, and nobody was told what they were for. In actual fact they worked just to get rid of some of their energy. Others had to fill in the trenches within a week or so, and then the men had to dig more of them. If the boys worked hard and long enough, other urges didn't come so frequently.

Other more cerebral means were devised to keep the troops occupied, and the short-lived Changi University came into being. An army can always produce experts in a variety of fields, not necessarily connected with their military service. Captain Adrian Curlewis:

> Within four days of the capitulation, Brigadier Herbert Taylor was appointed as the 'chancellor' of the university and I was appointed Dean of the Faculty of Law and general organiser. It was amazing the response we got from the troops – they all wanted to learn. We had representatives who could lecture on Tutankhamen in Egypt, on history, languages, mathematics, engineering and art. I personally took up the Malay language and motor engineering. We had plenty of what we called 'bomb-happy' vehicles to pull to pieces. But the paper shortage was simply terrific. We made blackboards, and used clay from a nearby pit for chalk.

Officers discovered that hundreds of the Australian troops were illiterate, and basic courses were organised to teach them to read and write. Some 400 joined these classes. One of the specialist courses amazed Russell Braddon, who remained incredulous over a self-improvement class he happened upon:

> Alec Downer [later Sir Alexander and a member of the Australian Federal Parliament] suddenly decided that he really couldn't bear any longer the way Australians spoke. He assembled a class of hairy, uncouth, pig-headed, very volatile Australian privates. They were thieves of the first water, and they survived because of their daring and recklessness. They used to sit on logs in front of Alec Downer while he conducted a litany of elocution, 'How now brown cow'! It was magnificent. Nobody sent them up. Nor did they send up Alec. But it was weird.

There was an unexpected bonus from the Japanese, who allowed in gramophone records and books supplied by the YMCA in Geneva. Other books were obtained by troops who sneaked through the wire to trade at night. The library was built up to some 20,000 books!

George McNeilly, a professional singer, began some musical appreciation classes in the open air at night:

> Men sat on the grass all around the huts. For some of the concerts, when I played jazz records for instance, I had an audience of 10,000. The music seemed to just float over the air into the night, and the boys really loved it.

There were even opera appreciation classes. Sergeant Stan Arneil recalled that some of them became quite expert when the music and plots were explained. Most were labourers and truck drivers. It is estimated that audiences of 3,000 turned up for George's classical music concerts. George Sprod:

> The troops all wanted swing records. Every time McNeilly would announce a record he'd put on his priestly voice and say, 'It don't mean a thing if you ain't got swing!' And the troops would sing out, 'rubbish rubbish'! George would then announce, 'Now as a special treat you're going to have a Christmas Oratorio by Johann Sebastian Bach.'

Live concerts by the Changi Concert Party began as early as the second day of captivity. First it was just individual performers, but soon evolved into a group of about thirty people. The Japanese liked coming to performances, and allowed the prisoners to build a theatre with teak boards on coconut stumps for seats. The army electricians improvised stage lights, and amazing coloured backdrops were painted using coloured clay dug from various depths of the latrine bore-holes – before they were commissioned of course. The Concert Party performed old favourites, but composed their own material. Particular favourites were 'Waiting for Something to Happen', and sentimental ballads about separated loved ones:

> I'll always remember the day
> The moment before you sailed away
> I feel sad and lonely
> But I think of you only
> While I'm waiting and praying for you . . .

Eating rice, Selarang

Getting used to the eternal diet - rice. Sam Solway is facing the camera and Jock McKenzie is standing at the rear eating from his dixie.

The Changi Concert Party performed almost right through the captivity, until the Japanese closed it down early in 1945. There were no women, of course, and the female impersonators were popular. Some men were given permission to grow their hair long. Others, like Keith Stevens, always burlesqued it up with a shocking red wig pretending to be a dumb sheila. But not all the female impersonators did so. Slim de Gray:

> All army concert parties had female impersonators and they were a big joke. I mean every time a guy came on in a dress the audience would yell and say, 'Ho Ho, look at him!' But

as time went by in Changi, the female impersonators became more and more conscientious about their make-up and they would not burlesque their roles. After a while you looked upon them as women. You knew that they weren't, but in the particular show you'd accept them. You'd say, well that's the girl. You wouldn't laugh at her, and she would look rather attractive.

Sports-mad Australians played football – Australian rules, rugby league and union – for one season only in Changi. All football (except soccer) was abruptly banned on 19 January 1943 by the Allied administration because of the violence and injury caused by the rugby codes. Soccer continued throughout the captivity until lack of food and energy ended it. Geelong was on top of the sports ladder when the axe fell, and so won the Premiership. Corporal L. A. 'Peter' Chitty was awarded the only 'Changi Brownlow Medal' ever presented.

Cricket was popular in the early days on the Changi Peninsula. Test matches, no less, were played against 'the old enemy', the British. A number of tests were played until 1943, when the work parties began to leave for the Thai–Burma Railway. Australia did rather well in these test matches. Lesser sports were basketball, tennis and boxing. It is remarkable that any sport was played at all in the extreme work camps on the Thai–Burma Railway, and in the early days at Sandakan before the death marches, where any excess energy had to be carefully husbanded by the skeletal and starved POWs. Sometimes the Japanese guards joined in a basketball game, or watched curiously. But bashings could happen at any time.

At Tonchan camp on the Thai–Burma Railway, Major 'Roaring Reggie' Newton of the 2/19th Battalion struck up a curious relationship with his Japanese overseer, an equally rambunctious and forceful character, Sergeant Major 'Tiger' Hiramatsu. The two men respected each other, and 'Roaring Reggie' was able to look after his men, while still allowing a reasonable work schedule – most of the time anyway. The bonus was, when conditions were dire, the 'Tiger' at least kept other guards from bashing 'Roaring Reggie's' men. At Tonchan, an English soldier, L. B. John happened to be a pretty handy professional boxer, and on a rare rest day, was asked to give a sparring demonstration. As he did so, with a fellow POW, Hiramatsu took an interest and told John to teach his Korean guards to box. This was awkward, as the Korean guards were only just above the prisoners on the Japanese hierarchical totem pole, and were feared by the Allied POWs as the most brutal guards on the railway. As John boxed fairly carefully with one of the Koreans, fearing reprisals later if he was too robust, the 'Tiger' intervened and told John to get stuck into him. John knocked the fellow out with one punch, and a delighted Hiromatsu organised another exhibition later during which John knocked out eight of the Koreans in quick succession! Whether there were reprisals is not known.

In the early days in Singapore, not everyone was in Changi. Some Allied POWs were quartered at Adam Park, labouring on a war memorial to the Japanese dead – not a task that filled them with great enthusiasm. Savvy Queenslanders were quick to locate termite colonies, and seed matchboxes full of them in the wooden base of the memorial. At Adam Park there was more opportunity to move about and scrounge; George Aspinall discovered a room in one bomb-damaged house full of confiscated radios, and managed to souvenir two. One he put into immediate service in a half-ruined house, conveniently operating on mains power and a time switch organised to coincide with the BBC news. One radio ended up in Changi Gaol, and the other was broken down and installed in a broom, and taken to the Thai–Burma Railway where it was never located by the Japanese.

Adam Park was only one of the temporary camps near the Singapore docks where Australians were housed while they unloaded all the British stores stacked in the 'godowns', as the big warehouses were called, and loaded them in ships bound for Japan. At Adam Park the POWs were quartered in a deserted village. Hugh Clarke and his group had more bizarre accommodation:

> About 500 of us were taken into the Great World, one of three massive amusement parks, the New World, the Happy World, and the Great World. The guard said, 'Right, there's your home,' so we just spread around and I ended up in a beauty parlour with three other blokes – in fact I slept in one of the showcases. There was a beer garden nearby, there was a theatre with a projection room. And of course we spread out like rats into every corner. We had a few electricians among us so very soon the camp was geared to electricity. I think we would have been using as much electricity as the rest of the city. From there we went to work on the wharves.

The Australians were in clover, never again in their entire POW experience to have the opportunity to get their hands on so much contraband. Curiously enough, this came as a surprise to the Japanese, who despite their contemptuous and often cruel behaviour to captured troops – who they thought were without honour because they should have committed suicide rather than surrender – were themselves scrupulously honest. Thieving would not have occurred to them. After captivity the Australians had also been made members of the Imperial Japanese Army, an 'honour' that sat fairly lightly on their shoulders. For men not getting enough to eat anyway, the godowns were both a larder and treasure house. Sergeant Frank Baker:

> There was an enormous amount of food on the wharves which the Japanese were taking away to Japan. They took loads and loads of beer – and they took a lot of empty bottles incidentally – from those wharves. We made hay while the sun shone. But one day there was something like eight heads of various Asian thieves displayed around Singapore. They were there as a warning to the population. To make sure we knew, they marched us just past the head that was at Singapore Railway Station, just opposite the wharf gates. Strangely, that day probably more stuff went out than on any other day. I think most of the fellows worked on the assumption that the Japs wouldn't bother to search – they would reckon we would be too scared.

Sometimes the Japanese themselves were uncertain about the nature of the goods in the godowns. Alex Drummond had what he considered a good win by convincing one gullible guard that

Laxettes, chocolate squares laced with senna, were 'No 1 *makan*' (food) and convinced him to eat a whole tin.

One of the problems smuggling goods out was the lack of clothing in which to hide the contraband, as the troops wore only a pair of shorts and a digger hat, or hat and a loin cloth, all that was necessary in the full tropical heat. Many a can of condensed milk, bully beef or cigarettes left the docks concealed in those high-brimmed hats. The art of concealing stuff under a loin cloth became known in the trade as 'crutching'.

It was quite remarkable what could be 'crutched' into camp. Dr Lloyd Cahill recalled that one expert in this practice actually crutched a live chicken into camp past the guards at the gate. My personal accolade for full honours in the noble art of crutching goes to one Private 'Snow' Peat, who managed to crutch home a pineapple:

> I got this small sized pineapple. I pushed it right down into my crutch, in between my legs. Anyway we marched back to Changi and I was bow-legged all the way, ripped raw and sore. I got the pineapple home, and six of us had a feed out of it, just added it to the rice. It was most delicious. It was well worth the effort.

Such small victories were eclipsed by a serious crisis in Changi which broke on the camp without warning on 31 August 1942. The Japanese presented Allied leaders with an ultimatum – every prisoner in Changi must sign a document agreeing that they would not attempt to escape. As it is the right of any prisoner of war to escape, the officers refused to sign. On the night of 1 September, the Japanese ordered that every prisoner of war assemble in the Selarang barracks square.

There were then 15,400 Australian and British troops remaining in Changi, and they all crammed themselves into the square measuring only 240 by 120 metres, with what personal gear and food they could carry. There were two water taps to service the whole area. Fred Stringer, a member of the Changi Concert Party, was there:

> It was men upon men upon men. Practically every square inch of the ground was covered with fellows and makeshift tents. Those who happened to be under cover were lucky.

Gangs of men dug latrines through the asphalt and a temporary hospital was erected. While the prisoners were moving into Selarang, Lieutenant Colonel Fred Galleghan, the senior Australian, and other Allied officers were instructed to go to Changi Beach. On arrival they found they were to witness an execution. Either out of perversity or nervous indecision the Japanese kept shifting the position of the victims, the firing squad and the spectators. At last Lieutenant Okasaka was satisfied. The four men facing the rifles included two Australians, Corporal R. E. Breavington, and Private V. L. Gale. Both had attempted to escape, suffered extreme deprivation, been recaptured, and returned to Changi. The men refused to be blindfolded.

Breavington turned to Galleghan and said, 'Goodbye, Sir, good luck,' and Lieutenant Okasaka signalled to the Indian riflemen to fire by waving his handkerchief. But the macabre drama was not over. At the first volley at least three of the men were wounded only. After another five or six shots Breavington shouted, 'For God's sake shoot me through the head and kill me.' The Indians fired another ten shots before Okasaka ordered them to stop. Through an interpreter a Japanese colonel said, 'The Japanese army does not like to put to death prisoners but unless you obey orders you must be put to death.' The Allied officers were ordered into trucks and driven back to Selarang.

They returned to a dire situation in the square, as men queued endlessly for water, and the outbreak of dysentery in this mass of humanity was only a matter of time. Sid Piddington (a member of the Changi Concert Party who specialised in a mind-reading act) was approached by 'Black Jack' Galleghan:

> He said to me, 'We'll put on a concert tonight.' I said, 'Where?' He said, 'In the middle of the square.' So we built a platform out of bits of wood and things and we put on this concert, the largest audience we ever played to, 15,400. They couldn't get away! By this time the Japanese had machine-guns and mortars surrounding the square in case there was any attempt to break out. At the end of the concert Black Jack walked up to me, I was then the stage manager, and he said, 'Play the King.' So the orchestra struck up the King, and over 15,000 sang 'God save the King'. I think it was one of the most moving moments I can remember in Changi. It stunned the Japanese.

Faced with the certainty of an epidemic, the Allied officers agreed to sign, having first got the Japanese to agree that they were ordering the prisoners of war to do so, thus making it clear the prisoners were signing under duress. George Aspinall said many wrote fictitious names, 'like Bob Menzies, Jack Lang and the old favourite Ned Kelly was mentioned many times'.

On 5 September, the men were allowed to return to their former quarters. Contrary to Japanese expectations, the whole crisis had boosted morale in standing up to their enemy. The signatures meant nothing.

Old concerns returned, like getting enough to eat and the troops' waning libido. Alex Drummond:

> A doctor gave a lecture early in the piece on the fact the prisoners might lose their fertility if they were long enough on the diet they were getting. After the lecture he asked, 'Has anybody got any questions?' One bloke said, 'Would you know of anything around the Changi area that would give us the vitamin C to ward this off?' The doctor thought about it, and he said, 'Well there's the hibiscus hedge around the camp. If you eat the leaves, that would help.' The next day it looked as though a plague of locusts had been through the hedge.

In August 1943 the Japanese made a significant move to alter the Allied command of the prisoners of war in Singapore, removing all the officers of the rank of full colonel and above from Changi. They were moved to isolated camps in Manchuria, where most survived the war. The senior officers then remaining in Changi were the commander in charge of the Australians, Lieutenant Colonel

F. G. Galleghan, and Lieutenant Colonel Holmes, who commanded all the British troops.

Galleghan, later to be Sir Frederick, was always 'Black Jack' or 'The Old Man' to the troops. A strict disciplinarian with a fine record in both world wars, Black Jack was a hero to his beloved 2/30th Battalion, but many other prisoners of war had a more ambivalent attitude to him. There was no doubting his courage and forcefulness. Twice wounded on the Western Front, he returned from World War I as a sergeant and was bitter about having been denied a commission.

That had changed by the outbreak of World War II – he served in the militia between the wars and was a lieutenant colonel by 1932. In 1940 he was appointed commanding officer of the 2/30th Battalion and immediately threw himself into strenuous training, which paid off when, on 14 January 1942 at Gemas, Malaya, he pulled off a brilliant ambush of a superior Japanese force, followed by a copybook withdrawal, for which he was awarded the Distinguished Service Order. Known as 'Black Jack' because of his dark complexion, black hair and piercing brown eyes, he was a formidable figure, six feet tall with a rock-like countenance and a military bearing that radiated command. Author David Griffin, a Changi veteran himself, wrote that a junior officer had summed it up well when he said, 'We were far more frightened of B.J. than the Japanese.'

Another author, Russell Braddon, who was captured in Malaya and had begun his captivity in the far-from-salubrious Pudu Gaol in Kuala Lumpur, was eventually transferred to Changi. He found Changi a pleasant alternative, almost unbelievably so:

Sports meeting on the Batu Pahat Padang
Our CO 'Black Jack' Galleghan (second from left) talks with two Australian Army nursing sisters.
From left, Sister Balfour-Ogilvy and Sister Kinsela.

In the fancy dress days of Changi, when it was a holiday camp with its university courses and everything else, Galleghan went so far as to issue an order that other ranks who had walking shoes would surrender them to officers – they were suitable garb for officers only. Officers must have two pairs of short pants, two pairs of long pants – I can't remember the exact numbers, but it was a handsome wardrobe. Ostensibly it was so they would appear to be properly dressed as officers and gentlemen. Those clothes had to come from other ranks who had carried them seventeen miles into Changi. They were confiscated – there was no question of being able to hide them.

Galleghan was as sincere as he was conceited and vain. He was like the monarch at the trooping the colour. He became quite hysterical if he were denied by anyone, even officers, the military courtesies. He was in many ways egomaniacal, and although brave and conscientious, destructive.

And yet that same man, and I have little to say about him that's flattering, was the one who did the most valuable thing for all men who came back from Thailand. We were a whingeing mob then. Cholera has a side effect which is a kind of melancholy. We all had it in a way. We had been more ill-done by than any other group of men in the world, and we wouldn't let those who had not been north forget it. Suddenly Black Jack got the majority of us together and said he knew we'd had a rough time, and we knew we'd had a rough time, but it was time to forget it and stop whingeing. It was extraordinarily salutary. But whilst that is a plus, there are many minuses.

Although he had commandeered the other ranks' clothes for his officers, Galleghan clearly gave himself no extra privileges with food. His weight dropped from 15 stone when he went into Changi, to 9 stone on his release. In 1971, shortly before he died, Galleghan at last responded to Braddon's criticisms.

We were able to continue in all the years to run Changi as an army. I know that I got criticised. You've got Russell Braddon who wrote *The Naked Island*. Russell Braddon's idea of how to run the camp was that it was to be like a town council, in which the mayor would be elected and all the rest of it. After all Russell Braddon was a private. I ran it totally differently. I ran it as if we were still in the army. I remember I used to say to the troops as often as I could, 'You're soldiers, and when I march you out of this camp I'm going to march you out as soldiers. I'm not going to march you out as a mob. You'll still be soldiers on the day it's over.'

A large number of Australians captured by the Japanese after the capitulation on 9 March 1942 never reached Changi. Of the 3,000 Australians in Java, most were to spend the next three or so years in camps in Bandung and Batavia (now Jakarta). Those who did make it to Changi, like 'Weary' Dunlop's force, were only there in transit to work on the Thai–Burma Railway. The survivors of the US cruiser *Houston*, and 300 Australians on HMAS *Perth*, sunk in the Sunda Strait on 28 February 1942, had begun their captivity stark naked, covered in fuel oil, after having been in the oil-fouled water from seven to fifteen hours. The Japanese gave them shorts and shirts, but no shoes. At least those who marched into Changi after the surrender had what they could carry.

Dunlop and his 900 men arrived in Changi from Java on 7 January 1943. After almost a year in harsh camps in the Netherlands Indies, they had very little. Many were barefoot. If Dunlop expected any help from Black Jack Galleghan in Changi, with his comparatively well-stocked Q Store, he could forget it. Galleghan was appalled by the men of Dunlop Force, who were not only dressed in rags, but neglected the niceties of saluting superior officers, which irritated him almost beyond measure.

Someone, probably on Galleghan's staff, dubbed the newcomers the 'Java Rabble', a name they wore with pride. A witty Java prisoner shot back with his description of the Changi lot as 'The Malay Harriers', marking their rapid defeat and retreat down the Malay Peninsula during the action. The 2/3rd Machine Gun Battalion historian commented: 'It was not the basis for friendly relations between troops of the AIF.'

As a surgeon with army rank, Dunlop was technically not a 'combatant' soldier. But his exceptional leadership in the camps of Java had naturally elevated him to lead Black Force.

Galleghan, who had taken an instant dislike to Dunlop and the Java Rabble, asked him what he could do to help. 'Give them clothes,' Dunlop replied, but Galleghan said there was not much to spare. Unbeknown to Dunlop, Black Jack also had plans to strip Dunlop of his command. He prepared a memo:

> Com. AIF desires following information:
> Name of senior combatant officer with party.
> Suggest changing OC party to combatant officer.
> Is there any reason for not making change?

Weary got wind of this and informed Brigadier Arthur Blackburn VC, who had also arrived from Java and who, after the departure of all other senior officers to Manchuria the previous year, was now the most senior Australian officer in the South-East Asian theatre.

Blackburn, about to leave Changi, was annoyed about Galleghan's memo, and wrote a reply, which he gave to Dunlop.

> I have considered this matter and desire Lieutenant Colonel Dunlop to retain command for administrative and disciplinary purposes so long as the troops brought over by him remain as one body.

Weary trousered Blackburn's letter, and waited his moment. That came at a formal dinner at the AIF headquarters in Changi shortly after Blackburn had left:

> Early in the evening, someone ill advisedly referred to 'the Java Rabble' and Weary shot to his feet in defence of the men under his command. He reeled off battles and places at sea, on land and in the air in which 'the troops that you refer to as the Java rabble' had fought. The battles spat out of Dunlop's mouth like 'a roll of drums'. The Battle of Britain, the Atlantic, Mediterranean, Western Desert, Greece, Crete, Syria, and Java . . . he was 'cutting, sarcastic, angry', and finished with a toast: 'And now we, the Java Rabble, salute you, the 8th Division, who fought so gallantly here in Malaya.' Blackburn would have loved it.
>
> After dinner, Galleghan took Dunlop aside, telling him he intended to go ahead with his intention to strip him of his command. Dunlop casually delivered Blackburn's note. After a pause, Galleghan, shocked, said Blackburn had no right to issue such an order.

Ten days later the Java Rabble left for the Thai–Burma Railway with Dunlop as their leader, thanks to Blackburn's intervention. Weary Dunlop became the most admired of the medical officers on the railway, saving many men's lives.

Dunlop and Galleghan parted on bad terms. Weary kept asking for boots and clothes for his 878 men, but Black Jack responded with six pairs of size 11s, a score of caps, 150 pairs of socks, and a dressing-down about his troops' poor marching. On his departure, Dunlop wrote to Galleghan:

> Two weeks ago my men arrived in a pitiful condition in this camp from Java. You have done nothing to alleviate their needs. Tomorrow at 8.30 they leave in the same pitiable condition, bootless and in rags. You have done nothing.

THE RAILWAY OF DEATH

WEARY DUNLOP AND BLACK FORCE WERE IN TRANSIT THROUGH CHANGI ON THEIR WAY TO Thailand, where it was rumoured there would be work camps, but probably better food. This myth was fostered by the Japanese. Geoff O'Connor recalled, 'It was going to be a land of milk and honey, plenty of food and very little to do.' Dr Kevin Fagan was told that, 'We were going on a holiday camp, good food, bring the pianos and musical instruments.' The reality was so unspeakable that the POWs would not have believed it had they been told.

Early in 1943, various work groups started to leave Changi. B and E Forces went to Borneo (the unluckiest destination of all). Dunlop Force left in January, followed by D Force, F Force, H Force, and smaller groups followed through the year.

The prisoners were unknowing builders of an ambitious railway project, designed to provide a supply line to Japanese forces in Burma, already feeling the strain of Allied attacks on their shipping in the Bay of Bengal. It would run from Ban Pong in Thailand through jungle and mountains to Thanbyuzayat in Burma – a distance of

38

423 kilometres – and was to be built in less than a year to support an offensive into India from Burma by Japanese forces in the next dry season. A huge work force of Asian labourers and Allied POWs was to build this link through rain, and very little shine, working non-stop on starvation rations and with primitive hand tools. One POW later commented that the elephants, brought in to do some heavy lifting, were better than men at demonstrating that if they did not eat they did not work.

Harsh realities were soon evident when men destined for the northern Burma end of the railway were crammed onto tramp ships in Singapore Harbour, in unbelievable numbers and squalor. They sat between decks, their knees drawn up with no room even to lie down to sleep. Sardines in a tin had a better deal. Jim Richardson:

> When we were stationary, it was hot. The perspiration just welled out on your body and face, and it even ran into your ears. I never thought it was possible to have anything like it. Diarrhoea was pretty rife, and if you wanted to relieve yourself you had to go up a vertical ladder and get out over the side. Of course a lot of the time you didn't make about the tenth rung, and down she'd come. You kept going and left the lot behind. Shocking it was.

After twelve days of this, the physical condition of the men was such that they could barely stand, let alone start to construct a railway. But common sense in nutrition and health for a more efficient work force was not part of the Japanese way of doing things. Eight Australians who attempted to escape after they arrived were

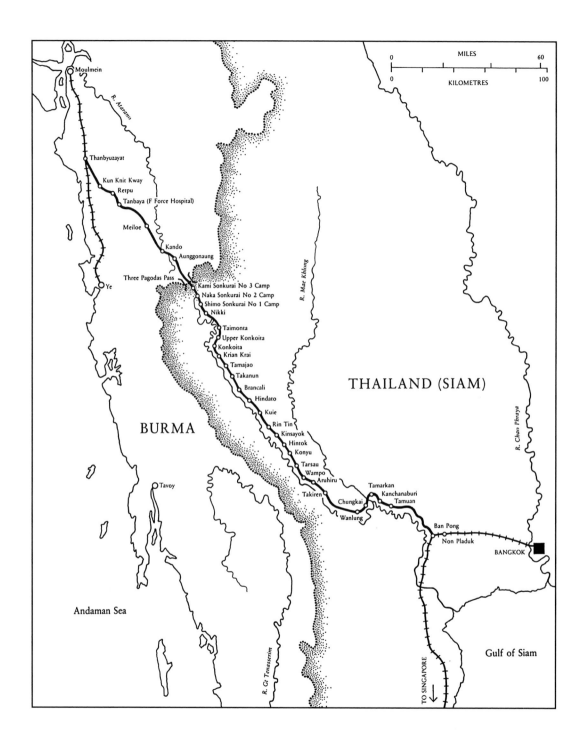

The Thai–Burma Railway

betrayed by local people, and summarily shot into open shallow graves in the jungle dug by their colleagues in heavy tropical rain. The holiday camps were not to be.

The prisoners labouring on the Thai side were little better off. After being herded into sealed railway wagons normally used to carry cattle, they were transported to Ban Pong, the beginning of the railway, and force-marched up country to build the work camps from which they would operate. Like their counterparts in Burma, these men began work on the railway in a debilitated state. One in three Allied prisoners would die working on the Thai–Burma Railway. The number of Asians, (known as 'romusha' from Burma, Thailand and the Netherlands Indies), tricked into joining the work force and with little or no organisation, died in their thousands – the number of dead has never been established. One estimate was over 100,000.

Equipped with wicker baskets and hoes (known as chunkels) the workers were told to dig cuttings and move the spoil to raise embankments for the line. Rickety bridges were built by criss-crossing timbers as supports, which the Australians made sure were liberally laced with termites. Just about everyone contracted dysentery or had malaria, or unnecessary diseases like 'wet' beriberi (where a man's legs and body filled up with water, sometimes doubling his body weight). Australian and British doctors, without any drugs, had to return to an early era of medicine to try to treat their patients. Crushed charcoal was all that could be found for dysentery patients. When cholera struck, in the height of the wet season, saline intravenous drips were improvised with stethoscope tubing and copper pipes from abandoned truck engines. Tropical ulcers had to be scraped

F Force men leave Selarang for the Burma Railway
By hiding myself on the second floor of one of the barracks buildings I was able to photograph our blokes being trucked to the Singapore Railway Station.

out with sharpened spoons, and in extreme cases led to amputation with partial or sometimes no anaesthetic.

The main problem was starvation. The greatest atrocity committed by the Japanese against the prisoners is that they did not feed them. In 1941, the army ration per man was 4,220 calories. They could survive and do some work on 3,000. In Changi they had been getting 2,000, and at that level they had been losing weight and suffering from deficiency diseases. On the railway they received even less, some watery stew, a few grains of rice and an occasional flavouring of meat and fish. To do hard labouring work on this meagre ration was to many a death sentence.

When the Japanese decided that the railway was not being built fast enough, they introduced periods of non-stop work with no rest periods, called 'speedos'. Ray Parkin remembers a Japanese officer passing on the instructions of the Imperial General Headquarters in stark terms:

> He gave a long speech and said we were doing a good job and the railway was progressing, but the railway must be completed – 'Nippon very sorry, many men must die'. Well, that began at least 150 days without a day off.

The already exhausted men were subjected to new extremes of brutality and punishment while the speedos continued. If the designated work quota could not be found, the sick were dragged out of the so-called 'hospitals' to make up the numbers. Stan Arneil:

> If they wanted 200 men, they had to have 200 men. The guards would deliver 200 men even if perhaps 30 of them might be on the backs of their mates. In the rain. So when we got there, if the beriberi was excessive, you might have to lie some of them on their backs with their feet against the side of the embankment to keep the fluid flowing down through the legs into their bodies so their legs wouldn't burst. They couldn't work at all. We'd feed them at lunchtime when we had a break. They were looked after, hats placed over their faces to keep the rain out, and they were talked to and joked

to. They understood the position. We would carry them back at night. Usually one would die during the day.

Sometimes the Japanese carried men on their stretchers to the work site where they were required to hold a rock-drill vertical while another two POWs hit it with a sledge-hammer. One of the worst places to work was known as Hellfire Pass, which had to be hewed out of solid rock. Hugh Clarke:

> It looked like a scene out of Dante's *Inferno*. The Japs decided we would work 24 hours a day, two shifts, one was the day shift and one was the night shift. Lighting became a problem but they are pretty resourceful people, and there's plenty of bamboo, so they formed a light party. Its job was to keep the fires burning all night. In addition to the bamboo fires, which threw a fair bit of light, there were some bamboo containers with hessian wicks and a bit of dieseline, and there were a few carbide lights. If you stood on top of the cutting, you would see the burning fires at intervals of about 20 feet – you'd see the shadows of the Japanese with their Foreign Legion caps moving round with their sticks belting men. We still had our slouch hats so you could distinguish the prisoners by being naked under the slouch hats, moving rocks around, hammering and clearing. There was shouting and bellowing. And this went on all night.

As Donald Stuart commented dryly: 'Dante knew less about infernos than we did. We could have given him lessons.' The Australian doctors were magnificent, working with practically nothing in the way of medicines or drugs. Ray Parkin, a survivor of HMAS *Perth*, had been with Weary Dunlop through Java, Changi and the Thai–Burma Railway:

> Weary's one of the great figures. He's like Mount Everest. You don't really see him till you stand well away. Up in Hintok we used to parade in the morning in the wet season – sick men and all had to turn out except those actually bedded down in hospital. The Japanese would select work parties from the fit men, then they would go for the next people, the so-called 'light sick', and they'd possibly send most of those out and then there were those that were doubtful. There was a huge log laid alongside the road, and the sick used to sit on it. We called it the wailing log. The Japanese would come along and they'd interrogate these blokes with a great *kurah*! Of course the first thing you did when you heard a *kurah* was to stand straight up to attention. If these fellows happened to stand up, they were fit enough to work. Weary told these men not to stand up in any circumstances – they were sick, and they couldn't get up. The Japanese would come along and say, *kurah*! The men would remain. Weary would go and pick up a man in his arms like a baby, bring him back over to Nippon, and say, 'This man, Nippon?' And then he would carry him back.

Unfortunately, as Weary himself said later, even this kind of gesture was meaningless in the long run in preventing the destruction of a third of the men, because the Japanese, 'Just sent the fitter men back and back to a relentless grindstone.'

Seriously ill men waiting outside 'hospital' hut
This water-damaged shot shows a group of men who can barely stand up, waiting to be inspected by a Japanese so-called doctor to see if they should go to work. They are virtually walking skeletons, and would all have had malaria, dysentery and beriberi.

The most feared disease was cholera, which – so the troops said – made dysentery look like constipation. Ray Parkin:

> One of the symptoms of cholera is a white stool. And I remember one day out on the line, I was sitting having my bit of rice upon the topside when a fellow came along and he squatted down just on the other side of the railway line to me. There was no false modesty out there, it was quite natural, in fact we were

all very clinical. This fellow looked down and saw a milk-white motion – and he saw that I saw it. He just gave me a look and it went right through me – it was the look of a condemned man. He knew he had it. He was dead the next morning.

The onset of cholera is dramatic, with intense cramps and fluid flows from every orifice. The eyes sink and the cheeks fall in as the dehydrated body 'shrivels up like a walnut'. Stan Arneil:

> We could tell within five minutes whether they had cholera. We would place a bamboo identification disc around their wrists with their regimental number and name on it because in four hours it was not possible to recognise a man who had contracted cholera.

Cholera was indiscriminate and often fatal, although the Australian doctors did manage to save many patients through heroic interventions with improvised drips. But a few men, overwhelmed with the situation they found themselves in, simply gave up the will to live. Optimism was as important as a wonder drug to the survivors. Roy Whitecross was in Burma:

> In my particular force of over 1,000 men, to my knowledge, there was only one who decided that to battle on was quite useless, and he one day sat with his rice from the midday meal and said, 'Anybody want any rice?' I said to him, 'What's the matter? Have you got malaria, are you crook?' He said, 'No, but do you want my rice?' I said 'You eat it.' 'No,' he said, 'no point. You battle on today and you're dead tomorrow.

You battle on tomorrow, and you're dead the next day. It's no bloody good.' Two or three of us got to him and we argued and we talked and we cajoled. We threatened to thump him, but it didn't do any good. He had just simply given up. About a week later he got a bit of a cold, it wasn't even influenza, it certainly wasn't malaria, and he promptly died. The rest of us never had any doubts that in the foreseeable future, a few months, we would be out. And that's what carried us through.

The railway was eventually finished, at horrendous and largely unnecessary loss of life that better organisation, even half-way adequate food and basic medicines might have averted. The casualty figures tell the whole sorry story. The Asian workers died and lay in unmarked graves, but without doubt topped the death toll. It is calculated that some 330,000 workers, including 62,000 prisoners of war, were employed on the railway. The Allied War Graves Registration units decided in 1946 that the number of dead among the POWs amounted to 12,399, including 6,318 British, 2,646 Australians, 2,490 Dutch and 589 unknown prisoners. Japanese engineers calculated they had built 4 million cubic metres of earth-works, shifted 3 million cubic metres of rock, and constructed 14 kilometres of bridgework, which was built in ten months.

By March 1944 most of the Australians had returned to Singapore. As George Aspinall commented aptly: 'It didn't take as many trains to bring the survivors back.' Those in Changi – which indeed seemed like heaven to the railway survivors – had known nothing of what had been taking place until their fellow Australians returned. Stan Arneil arrived back at Changi in a truck on 21 December 1943:

It was a moonlight night and Changi with the tropical waters around the island was so beautiful. I can still hear the squeal of the brakes as the trucks lined up. The people from Changi knew we were coming, and they came over to see us to look for old friends, and see how we were. We got out of the trucks, a couple were dead and we laid them on the ground, and we lined up on the road. We were not ashamed because we were soldiers, and we wanted to look like soldiers.

The people from Changi stood back and uttered not a word. It was really quite strange. We lined up on the road as best we could and stood up as straight as we could. Those who couldn't stand up straight were on sticks. And those who couldn't stop shaking with malaria were held by their friends. We thought this was what we should do as soldiers to say that we were not beaten. The sergeant major dressed us off, and we stood in a straight line as he went over and reported to Colonel Johnston.

Johnston went over to Black Jack Galleghan, and he said, 'Your 2/30th all present and correct, Sir.' And Galleghan said, 'Where are the rest?' The major – he was a major then – said, 'They're all here, Sir.' And we were. Black Jack Galleghan, the iron man, broke down and cried. It was an incredible scene. We wanted to show them we were soldiers.

THE SANDAKAN DEATH MARCHES

WHEN THE VARIOUS AUSTRALIAN WORK PARTIES LEFT CHANGI IN 1942, NOT KNOWING WHERE they were going, they had hoped that things might be a bit better than languishing on Singapore Island. Those who finished up on the Thai–Burma Railway had a horrendous time, but at least enough survived to speak of their experiences.

The 1,500 men of B Force who left in July, and 500 men of E Force who followed shortly afterwards, boarded the usual overcrowded 'hell' ships for a relatively short voyage to Borneo, where the Japanese planned to use them to construct an airfield at Sandakan on the north coast of the island. At first there was little indication that they were to be the victims of the most dastardly atrocity committed on prisoners of war by the Japanese in World War II.

At first their POW camp at Sandakan was tolerable by Japanese standards, although the work on the airfield was hard and unrelenting, accompanied by the usual bashings and lack of equipment to do the job. Under the Geneva Convention, Allied POWs were not supposed to work on projects involving military facilities, but the Japanese had signed but not ratified this convention, and ignored it.

Australians even found time, and were permitted, to perform amateur theatricals; food and cigarettes were unexpectedly better than expected; and the first year was looked back on as a bit of a golden age.

Finding they were near a town with people who were sympathetic to the ousted British, an underground network headed by Captain Lionel Matthews was organised through the remnants of the old British North Borneo Constabulary to smuggle extra food and medicines in to the Sandakan camp, and even components to build a radio receiver – and work had begun on a transmitter as well. The Japanese remained oblivious to all this, until early in July 1943 disaster struck. Lieutenant Rod Wells had built the radio receiver and was working on the transmitter:

> An Indian blackmailed a Chinese who was helping us in our general intelligence work. The Chinese refused to help the Indian – I think he wanted money – and the Indian told the Japanese. As a result of that two or three of our trusted Asian helpers were arrested. During the interrogation, unknown to us, Lionel Matthews' name was mentioned.

Wells and Matthews were taken away and interrogated under torture by the feared Japanese secret military police, the *Kempeitai*. Of the twenty-two Australians interrogated over the next four months, Matthews was executed, one man died, one was acquitted and the rest were sent back to Singapore to the military punishment prison of Outram Road Gaol, a former 19th century British-built gaol for Asians, holding inmates in tiny cells in solitary confinement with starvation rations. It did, however, save the lives of men who managed to endure this, who otherwise would have been slaughtered on the death marches that took place in late 1944 and early 1945.

The Sandakan camp, commanded by the sadistic six-foot-tall (183 cm) Captain Susumi Hoshijima, had lost enormous face over the underground network that had been operating unbeknown to him. The good days at the Sandakan camp were over. To add insult to injury, there had been four escape attempts. One group of escapers succeeded in crossing from Berhala Island (near Sandakan) through the Sulu Islands to guerrilla-held territory on Mindanao in the southern Philippines. Hoshijima decided that the Sandakan prisoners would be less trouble without their officers, and shipped all but five to Kuching in Sarawak, where they spent a comparatively benign time till the end of the war. They also missed the death marches, but later suffered agonies of guilt post-war, knowing that they had not shared their men's fate.

Life at the camp became grim. Keith Botterill:

> No more talking to the natives. Double the guard around the wire. Put out trained savage dogs to guard around the wire. Cut the rations and medical supplies. And we were still doing it hard at the aerodrome. The work parties were bashed along all day for no reason whatsoever.

Nelson Short, one of the survivors, remembered the Japanese were watching all the time. They were walking around with sticks like swords, and whacking everyone they didn't think was working hard enough. Short was punished, like many others, by being forced to stand up holding a heavy weight and looking at the sun. 'I got solar burns in both eyes.'

Dick Braithwaite:

> One fellow that was stood up outside the guardhouse for an unknown misdemeanour had his eye knocked clean out of its socket. There was no sympathy given for that at all. He was still kept standing there and he didn't get any treatment till he came back into the camp about six or seven hours later. There were numerous incidents of that nature. You tend to live with them and they don't stick in your memory because they were commonplace. As with the deaths it was a way of life that you learn to accept, and expected.

The Japanese also punished men by putting them in the *isho*, the cages. Built with slats of wood, the cages stood about a metre above the ground. The roof was too low for a man to stand, and they were too crowded to allow any man to lie down at night. Keith Botterill:

> The time I was in for forty days there was seventeen of us in there. No water for the first three days. On the third night, they'd force you to drink till you were sick. The first seven days you got no food. On the seventh day they started feeding you half rations. I was just in a G-string, never had a wash, and covered in lice and scabies. We were not allowed to talk, but we used to whisper. We had to kneel down all

day. There wasn't really room to lie down at night, but we all lay side-by-side, squashed up, and had to sit up again at dawn and kneel. Every evening we would get a bashing, which they used to call physical exercise. They'd bring us out at the set time of 5 o'clock every night. They had English cooks working for them because they wouldn't trust Australians anywhere near the cookhouse. The Englishmen knew that we got out at 5 pm so they'd come down then to feed the dogs with swill, the kitchen rubbish. They'd pour it into this trough. We all hit together, the dogs and all of us, and we'd fight the dogs for the scraps. If you've ever tried to pull a bone out of a starving dog's mouth, you'll know what it was like. The dogs would fasten onto your wrist to take the bone off you, and you'd still be putting the bone into your mouth. And you'd finish up the better.

In October 1944, Allied aircraft suddenly flew across the camp. The prisoners thought it was a prelude to invasion, but unfortunately for them, so did the Japanese. It is now known that before the atomic bombs were dropped on Hiroshima and Nagasaki and ended the war suddenly, there were secret orders that all POWs were to be killed in the event of an Allied invasion. The invasion did not eventuate, but in the meantime the Sandakan POW camp was attacked from the air. Nelson Short:

> The Japanese allowed us to put a big POW sign in black and white on the highest point. But the planes continued to bomb and strafe the camp. So the Japanese made us take

down the POW sign and give them an open go. Bombs left craters right in the camp and there was one just outside the camp that went right under a hut and killed twenty or thirty blokes. I can't understand it. When we had the POWs sign there, anybody could see it, and they just continued to strafe and bomb. The Japanese opened up on us as well. They were putting rifle fire into the camp. They were having a go too. They wanted to get rid of as many of us as they could.

By this stage there were some 2,000 Australians and 500 British POWs at Sandakan. By January 1945, the Japanese started to move POWs out of Sandakan, which was close to the coast, and march them inland to Ranau, an isolated camp 250 kilometres into the rainforests of North Borneo. Four hundred and seventy Australian and British prisoners were split into groups of fifty and marched into the jungle. Botterill, one of the six survivors, was with that first party:

> For the first five days we were going through mangrove and jungle swamps, and they made a path of logs. But we kept slipping off into the mud. So we decided to walk through the mud. The Japanese guards were doing that too – we were waist high, pushing through the mud. We thought if we fell from the logs and broke a leg they'd shoot us.
>
> You'd lie down of a night and you say, 'This is it.' Just in the swamps. The poor Japs were doing the same, you know. You lay up against a tree in the driest spot you could find, and you are that weary with aches, and 10,000 leeches as big

as pencils were climbing all over you. Off to sleep. Sort of sleep. Big baboons were screaming, wild pigs were making a noise and crocodiles. And I was twenty. I said, 'This is it. I'm going to die.' You could feel yourself dying. You'd sort of give up, and then you'd say, 'Oh no.' But you couldn't snap out of it. You just automatically got up, and away you'd go, you know. I never had a great will to live – I just put it down to luck. If you were all right in the morning, well, that was it. You could take the day as it came. Don't let the day beat you. Say, 'Well it's going to be a good day today. I know I'm there to get a couple of thumpings but that's all right. Just cop it. Don't let nothing get you down.' That's how I found it.

I've seen men shot and bayoneted to death because they could not keep up with the party. We climbed this mountain about 30 miles in from Ranau, and we lost five men on the mountain in half a day. They shot five of them because they couldn't continue. But I just kept plodding along. It was dense jungle, I was heartbroken, but I thought there was safety in numbers. I just kept going.

There was no respite in Ranau. The remnants of Botterill's group of fifty were given sacks of rice and told to carry them back towards Sandakan as food for the second party which would come later. It was partly moving food, but mostly a killing party. As the exhausted men could not go on, they were shot. Botterill was among the last in his group left alive, and sheltered in a small hut. Even in extremis, it was good to see the Australian entrepreneurial spirit alive and well. Botterill:

Because only half the men could eat curry, they would just give it to you in a small tin and you could please yourself what you did with it. Well, we used to trade curry to the Japanese 25 miles back at Paginatang. Now to double the quantity, we used to get the borer droppings out of the bamboo. It just looked like curry. We used to mix it, 50 per cent borer droppings and 50 per cent curry and traded with the Japanese for ice and salt. They thought they were on a good thing and we knew we were on a good thing.

Every night some of the exhausted men would die in their sleep.

There'd be a burial party every morning, approximately 9 o'clock, which consisted of two men to each body. We used to wrap their wrists and ankles together and put a bamboo pole through them and carry them like a dead tiger. We had no padre. And no clothes on the bodies, just straight into six-inch deep graves. The soil was too hard to dig any deeper.

In May 1945, the Japanese administration in Sandakan were preparing for what became known as the second death march. Death was stalking the camp anyway, with 230 British and Australian prisoners dying in the month of March alone. On 29 May, the Japanese ordered all the remaining Australians and British at Sandakan to parade. Only 566 prisoners were fit enough to muster, and they watched as the guards beat the sick to see if any of them could stand up and join the parade. Then they too were marched into the jungle. The second death march had begun. Ominously, as they left the camp it was torched, and they could only guess at the fate of the sick still there. Bombardier Dick Braithwaite said they saw the camp burning with a great sense of loss. It was the only home they knew. This time the wretched, starved men were soon in no doubt what awaited them. Braithwaite:

> I became aware it was a one-way trip when we started to hear shots, and you felt there was no hope for anyone that fell out. I was going up one of these slippery slopes one time, and not making much headway when I got a crack across the back with a rifle swung by the barrel, and I got a bit of a kicking. That's why I'm deaf in one ear now as a matter of fact – I got a rifle butt in the ear. Then another one came straight at my face, and fortunately I just turned otherwise it would have caved the front of my face in. But it just skidded off my mouth and mashed up my lips, so I didn't lose any teeth. I'm sort of semiconscious, as I recall, and I felt this fellow riffling through the old pack that I had. But they had used my rice so he couldn't get any of that. I was just lying there. I don't know whether you've had the experience of being in the water and becoming absolutely beat. You can't get your breath and you're gasping. You're just heaving, trying to get your breathing going. Or that's how I was. A group came past me, and Bob Sykes, who was a warrant officer in my unit, said, 'Come on son, you can make it.' And I said, 'Yes Bob, I'll be there.' Anyway after they'd gone past I struggled up on my knees, then up on my feet, and staggered on.

Nelson Short was in Braithwaite's group:

We'd only go on for a few yards and we hear the killing off party coming behind. And if blokes just couldn't go on, we shook hands with them, and said, you know, hope everything is all right. But they knew what was going to happen. There was nothing you could do. You just had to keep going yourself – more or less survival of the fittest. There was nothing you could do.

Private Keith Botterill, Bombardier Dick Braithwaite, Private Nelson Short, Gunner Owen Campbell, Lance Bombardier William Moxham and Warrant Officer William Sticpewich were the only survivors from 2,500 prisoners who began the death marches. They escaped by slipping into the jungle, eventually saved by local people who kept them alive until the invading Allied forces arrived. They were the only ones left who could describe what had happened. Sticpewich later gave evidence to the war crimes trials in Rabaul.

Perhaps the most unlikely survivors were those who had been tried after the underground network had been discovered, and sent to the punishment prison, Outram Road Gaol, in Singapore to serve their sentences in tiny cells in solitary confinement. At least they would miss the death marches. Because Outram Road was a *Kempeitai*-run institution, they were expected to serve their full sentences. This was impossible because of the meagre diet of rice and watery soup. So when it seemed death was inevitable, the skeletal and scabies-infected Outram Road prisoners were taken by truck and dumped outside the gates of Changi for them to be fed up and restored to health – in order to return to Outram Road to resume their suspended sentences. Rod Wells, who had made the secret radio in Sandakan camp, was one such case. Dr Glyn White at Changi recalls his condition when he came in:

> Well, Rod was unrecognisable. And you could count the surface anatomy of every bone he had in his body, practically, he was so emaciated. And almost too weak to talk. I was only about seven stone myself, but Rod, it was just like picking up a weenie little baby. I can still feel now how he relaxed as soon as I got him into my arms. It was a very emotional episode. He was almost too weak to speak. But you could see his smile under his whiskers.

THE MOVE TO CHANGI GAOL

UNTIL MAY 1944, 'CHANGI' HAD COME TO MEAN THE CHANGI PENINSULA, AND IN PARTICULAR for the Australians, the bomb-damaged Selarang Barracks, which was repaired and mains electricity put back on. There was plenty of room to move around, and even occasional visits to the beaches in the area to collect salt water to cook the rice or, on occasions, swim. But as the war dragged on, the Japanese became less obliging, and 11,700 prisoners, including 5,000 Australians, were moved in and around the Changi Gaol itself, which up to that time had been used to house civilian detainees. This is the 'Changi' that is best remembered as a hardship camp, as all this humanity was crammed into a quarter of a square kilometre. Rations were cut, camp life was much more restricted, and in July even the authority of Australian officers over their troops was revoked.

The role of the officers during captivity during the three-and-a-half years from 1942 to 1945 was in some ways controversial. In action, officers die (and did die) in greater proportion to the troops. But during the captivity this was reversed. The Japanese accorded the officers privileges, meagre but important. They were paid (in almost worthless occupation currency) more money than the other ranks, so they could buy extra food, but most significantly they were not required to do the hard physical work that the other ranks were forced to do.

This alone meant that being an officer as a prisoner of war of the Japanese was virtually a ticket home. Some did die, and others (particularly the doctors) did not spare themselves in caring for the prisoners, particularly on the Thai–Burma Railway. The officers who tried to intercede with the Japanese to get better treatment for their men were often bashed. Some, like 'Roaring Reggie' Newton of the 2/19th Battalion, copped the bashings and continued to attempt to guard the interests of their blokes until the end. Others tried once or twice and then gave up. Many of the officers started to think of survival and getting home themselves. And some individuals behaved disgracefully. George Aspinall was in F Force on the Thai–Burma Railway:

> There was one particular officer who was renowned for laying back all day doing nothing, issuing orders and making life very hard for the rest of the men that were working. To some extent he was co-operating with the Japanese to our detriment. The men detested this particular person. Even today they don't talk about such things publicly, they prefer to let bygones be bygones, but when a group is talking privately some of these names come up and there's a real hate session.

This man, Lieutenant Colonel C. H. Kappe, enraged Black Jack Galleghan when he came back fat from the railway. His men

View from train, Thailand

were skeletal. Bizarrely he was awarded an OBE after the war! Some officers on the railway pooled their officers' allowances and provided extra rations for their men. Don Moore recalls one self-serving officer with particular distaste:

> He was known as the White Jap, and he was entirely dedicated to his own self-preservation. He was affluent by POW standards. He had money that he would lend where he'd be paid double or three times the price in English currency when he came back. This money had come from the proceeds of

a canteen which he ran at the camp of which he was the commander. In this case, it was a private enterprise purely and simply for himself. This fellow I speak of has never been back to any reunion that I know of.

Happily these officers were the exceptions to the general rule.

Not all the prisoners returning from the Burma Railway stayed in Changi. The fittest were marched down to the Singapore docks and herded on to tramp ships for transport to Japan to work in coal and iron ore mines in a Japanese winter. The Japanese attempted to transport 4,000 servicemen to Japan at this time from the Pacific and South-East Asia.

Travel by sea was one of the most hazardous prospects for POWs. Some of these ships were sunk by American submarines on the way, with tremendous loss of life. A few lucky men were actually picked up by the submarines, who thought at first they were Japanese sailors in the water and were preparing to machine-gun them. Some had been clinging to wreckage in the warm tropical waters for up to six days. One was Arthur 'Blood' Bancroft (he had red hair) who was a survivor of the sinking of HMAS *Perth* in Sunda Strait. He was about to complete the full tour, Java, Changi, the Thai–Burma Railway and – but not for him – Japan. Other shipmates, like Ray Parkin, did finish their captivity in Japan, working in mines uncomfortably close to where the atomic bombs exploded. Some of the rescued men returned to Australia in 1944, bringing the first news of the harsh treatment of POWs on the Thai–Burma Railway and other camps.

Historian Hank Nelson wrote:

Travelling dispersed units. The 2/6th Field Company of Engineers was captured in Java. By the end of the war only ten men were still in Java. Others were scattered in Sumatra, Borneo, Singapore, Indo-China, Thailand and Japan. The 2/29th Battalion suffered in the fighting on the Malayan Peninsula and on Singapore, but had lost many more men after the surrender. The battalion dead were separated by thousands of kilometres. Men died with the communist guerrillas in Malaya, with A Force in Burma, with B Force in Borneo, with F and H Forces in Thailand, and others were buried or cremated in camps as far apart as Java and Japan. The prisoners were like debris in a flood. Some were dumped in backwaters, they were caught in eddies, detached from one group and linked with another – and they stayed in the mainstream while all around them sections were impeded and averted. When prisoners met, an immediate task was to trace movements of different groups and speculate on the whereabouts of other men from the unit.

Back in the new crowded Changi Gaol camp, it became more dangerous for the men operating the secret radios. Being caught was a certain death sentence. Don Wall, who had a background in intelligence, was in charge of one radio. Don would tune in to the BBC in the morning, and a colleague, Tommy Thompson, would take it down in shorthand and then type it out. It was agreed that no news would be released until after the working parties came back into the camp between 5 and 6 pm. That was the time the 'bore-hole' rumours floated about, and news could also notionally have been gleaned from sources outside the camp. The typed-out news bulletin was given to the Australian commander, Black Jack Galleghan. Don Wall became concerned that Black Jack was big-noting himself by releasing the news to a certain group of officers earlier in the day, which compromised security.

Don decided to put out a false story to test out his theory. 'So we put a rumour in the bulletin that Churchill had been killed in a plane crash in southern France. This was after the Normandy landings. It was around the camp in the morning, soon after Black Jack got it.'

(After the war, one of Galleghan's staff officers confirmed to Wall that Black Jack had been leaking the bulletins before the agreed time.)

Wall decided to close down the radio because of this security breach, and buried it in a secure, secret place. Black Jack was furious that he was cut off from his news bulletins, and according to Don Wall, did an unforgivable thing. At that time Don was working with a tunnelling party that was building air raid shelters for the Japanese into hills in the middle of Singapore Island. Wall:

> And I think it was Black Jack who told a Japanese officer that I was a person of interest. Three Japs came and got me, and they marched me down to the Jap office and Sargy was there. Now Sargy was the interpreter at Nikki on F Force, and I knew him pretty well.

Wall had been Sargy's driver on the Thai–Burma Railway, and fortunately for Wall, they got on well. As a result of the tip-off, the

Japanese had searched Don's quarters and found his diary – which of course POWs were forbidden to keep. Sargy's nickname for Don Wall was 'Driver':

> 'Driver, you can have this,' and he handed me back my diary. It didn't have anything hot in it. I took it back. Then he said, 'You may go.' Now someone, and I think it was Black Jack, told Sargy or someone of Sargy's rank, that I was a person of interest to get back on me for stopping his news.

Wall said he was extremely lucky that Sargy was the officer who dealt with him.

With the end of the war imminent – although the atomic bombs had not yet been dropped in Japan – there was a fear that trenches the prisoners had been forced to dig outside the Changi camp were to be their graves into which they would be machine-gunned in the event of an Allied landing. Certainly it can be argued that in the case of Sandakan, the vulnerability of the camp to the coast and an early Allied rescue mission may have triggered the death marches – perhaps an early example of the secret order regarding POWs being put into practice.

The POWs are in no doubt that the sudden ending of the Pacific War because of the atomic bombs saved their lives.

ALL OVER

been broadcast by Emperor Hirohito himself on 15 August – the voice of the divine emperor had never before been broadcast. But in POW camps from Timor to Manchuria the news trickled through slowly, and often the stunned Japanese were slow to let the POWs know they were free.

Charles 'Nutty' Almond was still in Thailand, working at a camp north from Ban Pong, the southern end of the Thai–Burma Railway:

> We worked a couple of days after the war finished. We came home from work one night and the flags were flying from all huts. The Japs had finally announced that the war was over. I wouldn't believe it. My mate said, 'The war is over, Chas.' And I said, 'Not again!' He said, 'It is fair dinkum this time.' I said, 'Yeah I'll believe it when I see it.' He said, 'Well come out here.' One of our chaps was walking along and there was

a Jap walking towards him. As they got close to each other
the Jap stuck out his hand, offering to shake hands, and our
bloke just hauled back and clocked him one under the chin.
I said, 'The war is over fair enough.'

At Changi, the prisoners were up with the latest news due to
the secret radios still operating. But they were still apprehensive
about how the Japanese would react, and believed that the Japanese
would be bad losers. Stan Arneil:

> There was a young [Australian] fellow dropped onto the
> aerodrome and he looked like a pirate. He must have been
> about six foot three inches. He seemed to be as wide as an
> ox, in great health, with a revolver and all the sort of thing,
> and he looked absolutely beautiful.

Chris Neilson, a survivor of Outram Road Gaol, was in Changi
receiving much-needed medical attention at the time of the surrender
and witnessed the same commando arriving:

> You would have thought he was Flash Gordon. He looked
> the part, he'd have given Flash Gordon a hiding. He strolled
> in among us and we all cheered like bloody hell. A Jap raced
> up to meet him. Evidently they had been told that he would
> be coming in on his own. This Jap came up, bowed and said,
> 'I will take you to Takahashi.' He was the head of Changi
> prison camp. This bloke just went whack. and lifted him
> under the chin. He said, 'You take me nowhere, you bring
> bloody Takahashi to me.' The Jap ran away and next minute

> Takahashi came at the double. Oh it was lovely! You should have heard us cheer. And here is Takahashi rushing and bowing, and this bloke upbraided him, slapped his face.

When more commandos arrived, they were astonished at finding an Australian Army frozen in time from 1939. During the war, rules had changed. Loose-fitting camouflage clothing was the order of the day and the inflexible rule of saluting an officer whenever you saw one was dead and buried. Saluting, blancoed webbing and shining brass buckles were still de rigueur under Black Jack's stern discipline. The outside world was to impinge in more ways than one.

Curiously enough, there was little enthusiasm for revenge against the Japanese. George Aspinall:

> There were a number of dead Japanese found at the back of Changi Gaol down at the beach. Whether they were shot by Chinese or by our people, we don't know. But we were so pleased, so elated that the whole thing was over and we would be going back home, I don't think a lot of us were looking for revenge.

Eddie Henderson agreed:

> Our old guards that ill-treated us were taken away and new guards brought in. The Japanese knew it was all over and probably wanted to avoid incidents. The Australian attitude, I think, is that you can't kick a dog while it is down and they looked so beaten and so subservient that we couldn't

do anything to them. But if they had been the ones that ill-treated us, we probably would have been into them.

But some POWs were literally killed with kindness in the days following the surrender. In Japan, American B29 bombers dropped food, not bombs on any POW camps they could locate. Hugh Clarke:

> The B29s circled the camp a few times and then came over again and made the drop. Each food container consisted of two 44-gallon drums welded together, and they dropped them with coloured parachutes, red, blue and green. As we looked up, the parachutes opened with a jerk, half the drums broke off and came hurtling down into the camp. I got my arms around the trunk of the tree. The medical orderly in the camp was a fellow named Joe Truey, an American. He got hit on the head with a case of Spam and was killed instantly. There were broken legs.

David Runge:

> Another American was standing up with his arms folded. The lid of a drum buried into his chest, cutting off both his arms and killing him.

Naturally all POWs wanted to get home quickly, but transport by air and sea in the immediate aftermath of the surrender was difficult . The Allied command created an organisation to expedite the returns, Repatriation of Allied Prisoners of War and Internees (RAPWI) which could not produce quick results with former prisoners in camps in Indo-China, Thailand, Burma, Java, Sumatra, the Netherlands East Indies, Ambon, and British North Borneo. About 2,700 were distributed between Japan, Korea, Manchuria and Hainan. Then there were nearly 6,000 Australians on Singapore Island and Johor in Malaya.

The frustrated ex-POWs immediately re-dubbed RAPWI – Retention of All Prisoners of War Indefinitely. Many did not get back to Australia until late October, from distant collection and assembly locations in a number of countries. In broad figures, 22,000 Australian servicemen and women had become prisoners of war of the Japanese. Only 14,000 came home.

Post-traumatic stress disorder is now a recognised condition, particularly for soldiers returning from war. The returning 8th Division men from South-East Asia had endured not only combat, but three-and-a-half years of treatment by their captors that can only be described as punitive and bestial. Apart from the malnutrition and tropical diseases that could claim their lives, there was daily uncertainty with the possibility of a random attack of brutality from a Japanese or Korean guard that could kill. They had all lived absolutely abnormal lives under enormous stress for nearly four years in an alien environment controlled by the Japanese whose approach to captured soldiers was uncaring and contemptuous. If any group of men needed counselling, they did. But to be fair, they didn't want it, and there was none available anyway. What they wanted was just to get on with their lives in Australia and make up for that lost time. Some managed it better than others.

The Australians survived the Thai–Burma Railway, and the slave labour camps in general, better than any other nationality.

Many of the British soldiers had arrived in Malaya recruited from the slums of the major cities, young, ill-trained, and not as healthy as the AIF lads. The Australians were often recruited from country towns, and had bush skills which enabled them to light a fire and boil a billy in a tropical downpour, or put up rudimentary shelters using a machete and their practical know-how. They were also very conscious of mateship, and in extremis, small groups of usually no more than three to five men looked out for each other. For example, when one of the group had malaria and could not eat his rice, his friends shared what he could not eat, but made sure they returned the favour when they too became sick.

The British class system was entrenched in their army. The British officers often did not have the rapport with their men that the Australians did – although clearly there were some who did. But probably because of the physical disparity between the English slum kids and the Australian bush boys, the British soldiers started with a disadvantage.

All the surviving Australian POWs agree that mateship was a key ingredient in their survival. And that endured to a great degree when they returned to Australia. Their experiences had been so extreme, so beyond the experiences of their families and friends at home, that a great many returning POWs simply didn't want to talk about it. But they could talk about it with their POW mates, and this became a great safety valve for those who could do so.

The actual experience of returning home could be traumatic. Many former prisoners had been twenty or so when they reached Malaya and Singapore. They were now 24, and had had little or no news from home in all that time. As Hank Nelson wrote:

They had missed the years when their vigour was at its greatest, when they would have played their best sport, when they would have selected a career, and when they would have married. They were all conscious of the distorted pattern in their lives. They felt a need to try and catch up, and some were uncertain that they could do so.

The excitement of actually reaching Australia made many returning prisoners unaware of their infirmities and how they looked to other people. One group flying home from Manila, via Morotai and Darwin, put down at an airfield in South Australia. An ex-prisoner whose legs had been amputated was carried piggy-back by his mates. All were joyous and confident. Don Moore:

> We were told we could go and have a stretch while they refuelled. And there was a group of ladies all lined up with these goodies. The cups of tea, cream cakes, everything that country hospitality could supply. We went over to them, smiling and happy – and they were all crying, just holding their heads down. We realised what we were, in their eyes, bloody scarecrows. We were figures of pity.

A favourite POW saying for men worried about the effects of their experiences on their virility and speculating on their home-coming was, 'And the second thing I'll do is take my pack off.' But four years is a long time, and for some it was not all moonlight and roses. Patrick Levy:

> Some men went back happily to the arms of their wives and children, some to their mothers, fathers and sisters, but I

didn't. I was not unhappy with my mother and my brother. My wife met me too, and then cleared out.

George Williamson:

I got a Dear John letter. She got word that I was missing in action, believed killed. And well, you can't blame her, can you? So then I got a divorce and that was that.

Rusty O'Brien:

Before we were sent back home we were going to get letters from home acquainting us of what was going on. If that had happened, there would have been less heartbreak. Lots of fellows came back to broken homes. One fellow shot his wife. Another fellow burnt himself after he shot his wife.

Many though, had happier homecomings. Sir Adrian Curlewis:

Our wives and families had all week been warned not to give prisoners too rich meals. They were to treat them very carefully because their stomachs wouldn't be able to take it. But somehow I got quite a good feed when I got home. And champagne. My wife had put the bottle away for three years and kept it for me.

Lady Curlewis:

And it didn't seem to affect him at all. And he just looked around and he said with a sigh, 'Oh, isn't it clean!'

Worries about virility were fortunately quickly banished as soon as the ex-POWs put on a bit of condition. Bob Yates:

> As far as the opposite sex was concerned, we were told that after our experiences we wouldn't be much good. But that's been proved wrong fortunately.

Daisy Sloane:

> We'd been told that we probably wouldn't be able to have a family for a while. We'd only been married the nine months and we had a baby boy, and then a couple of years later twin girls. So that wasn't too bad for the rice diet!

There were odd phobias for some men to overcome when they returned. Chris Neilson was a graduate from the awful Outram Road Gaol where prisoners were kept in solitary confinement and starved in small bleak cells for years. With plenty of food available for the asking, Neilson was unable to bring himself to take advantage of it:

> I know this, I couldn't go into a bloody cafe. If I was as hungry as buggery, do you think I can go in there and order a meal? Had to find some bugger looked like he was hungry and ask him to have a feed with me. I couldn't do it on my own.

Herb Trackson, another Outram Road graduate, also had problems:

> You always seem to be frightened of something. As far as my case goes, I could not bear to be on my own. I have to have

someone with me, or someone around me, even if it was strangers. To be in a room by myself was just impossible. I'd have to get out or make an excuse to go and see someone.

The world had changed in their absence. Some men found their jobs had been taken by others in spite of laws that should have given them security, or their skills were no longer in demand. Technical advances like jet propulsion were a big surprise, or the once stuffy ABC playing jazz music, or having Bing Crosby crooning away on Sydney's 2BL. Another revelation was how Australian women behaved. Jim Richardson:

> I was in a train and I watched this woman. There was a lot of smoking now. She pulled a packet of weed out, rolled it, licked the paper, put it in her mouth and said, 'Hey, soldier, have you got a match?' Oh God, I couldn't get over it. Rolling her own cigarette, and just turning around and biting me for a match. I said, 'Here, you can have that.' 'Oh, I don't want all your bloody matches,' she said. And the language of them!

Unable to talk of their experiences to friends or families, who just had no idea of what they had been through, the ex-prisoners sought out each other's company whenever they could – very often in pubs. At least they understood each other. Health was another issue. Just wanting to get on with life, they made light of chronic conditions. At the end of the war, medical officer Ian Duncan, who had worked not only on the Thai–Burma Railway, but in labour camps in Japan, interviewed every Australian and British soldier he could find in his last camp when the war suddenly ended, because he thought it his duty to record their disabilities. Duncan:

> And you'd say to them, what diseases have you had as a prisoner of war? Oh, nothing much, Doc, nothing much at all. Did you have malaria? Oh yes, I had malaria. Did you have dysentery? Oh yes, I had dysentery. Did you have beriberi? Yes, I had beriberi. Did you have pellagra? Yes, I had pellagra – but nothing very much. All these are lethal diseases. But that was the norm, you see, everyone had them. Therefore they accepted them as normal,
>
> I would say most of them, at least 50 per cent, had some form of nervous trouble. A lot of them had stomach trouble, a lot had gastric and duodenal ulcers, a lot had chronic diarrhoea long after the war. But everyone who worked, certainly on the railway and in the mines in Japan, had some form of arthritic degeneration caused by the conditions under which they worked. I've seen X-rays of the spines of some of these men, and they are really shocking – how they got around I don't know. But they did, and they made light of it. The men almost invariably came in and said, 'Well, I don't want to seem to be a bludger, but I've got this trouble . . .' Or, 'I thought I'd come along and see you, I don't think I deserve any pension, we didn't do much fighting.' And this was their attitude. They actually believed they were not entitled to a lot of the benefits of ex-servicemen. But they are. They fought a pretty hard war, as prisoners of war.

Making sense of it all remained a preoccupation with the ex-prisoners. I think the last words should be theirs.

Graham Chisholm:

> I am angry about the futility of it all. I'm angry when I go to the Commonwealth War Graves in Singapore and I look at the fine young men there under the pieces of slab, nineteen, twenty, twenty-one and twenty-two years of age, whose lives were sacrificed for no real reason. The slice out of my own life still leaves dark passages because those were vital years, and you're denied everything. But so were other people. We came out of it and we rehabilitated ourselves.

Army nurse Sylvia Muir:

> Out of my life I lost four years – and very valuable years when you're twenty-five to twenty-nine. They were certainly lost years except for the friendships I made there and the experience it gave me. I think it's made me more tolerant. Things that I used to worry about, now I couldn't care less. *Tidak apa* as the natives say.

Jack Panaotie:

> When we get talking together, we say, 'Couldn't go through it again, but we wouldn't have missed it.' An experience that we know that nobody else knows. Not that you wanted nobody else to know about it, but you cannot explain it to anybody else. Because we are unique.

PART II
George Aspinall's Story

'YOU'LL BE SORRY!'

I BEGAN MY MILITARY SERVICE AS A CADET IN THE 21ST LIGHT HORSE REGIMENT AT WAGGA IN 1939. My uncle, J. J. Quinn, had been a World War I man and he encouraged me to join. I was working on my uncle's property as a farm hand at the time and, as I was only sixteen, I was too young to be a permanent soldier. The unit I joined was known as Cadet Troop Headquarter Company. You had to provide your own horse and some equipment. The army supplied saddles. I used to go to various weekend troop outings at Wagga, and got to know a bit about army life in general because we had to do much the same sort of things as the permanent soldiers.

Although I wasn't tall, I was pretty wiry and fit, and I was considered a pretty good runner. I did well at most of the sports I participated in. In fact I was considered A1 in those days and my physical condition was as good as the next bloke . . . better than a lot.

I was still with my uncle when war broke out and, about the middle of 1940, a group of us with the 21st Light Horse decided to join the AIF. At seventeen I was still under age but I borrowed

My horse Tim at Matong
Tim and I joined the Light Horse in 1939.

my cousin Frank Quinn's birth certificate, which got me into the army. You see, the important thing was to pass the medical, and I went to the doctor using my cousin's name and his birth certificate. Then, when I went to the Sydney Showground to sign up, I gave my correct name and address and no one checked on my age because I had already passed the medical. In fact the army did not discover I had joined under another name until I came back from Malaya and Singapore after the war!

Things were pretty rough and ready at the Sydney Showground. We got off the train at Central and had to walk to the Showground. On the way, we passed groups of men marching . . . everyone seemed

Sturt Street, Wagga
One of my first photographs.

to be marching. Some were dressed in loose-fitting khaki jackets and khaki drill trousers, with cloth caps on their heads. We found out it was called a giggle suit. One group had wooden sticks on their shoulders which were supposed to be rifles. Every time we passed these marching men they would shout out, 'You'll be sorry!' That became the usual saying when a new group of recruits came into an army barracks area. There'd be a shout of, 'You'll be sorry!'

The whole of the Showground complex was being used in those days without much alteration. The pavilion I was in was used for the poultry display. You could certainly smell that chooks had been there. The chook pens had been moved out and replaced with rows

On the farm at Matong
Ten-horse team in action sowing wheat.

of beds . . . wire stretchers with straw-filled chaff bags as mattresses. Judging by the smell, the straw had come straight from the horses' stalls. We were told, 'You'll get a lot worse than this,' and we laughed at that . . . little knowing what the future held for us.

The discipline was strict, but I was used to the basics of army life because of my experience with the 21st Light Horse. I learned to settle down with the rest of my mates, because everybody wanted to get overseas. To get overseas you had to be well trained and disciplined, and that was always in the back of our minds.

After about six months of drill and basic training at the Showground, we thought we were getting pretty good, and it was all getting old hat. We'd been out to the Long Bay rifle range several times and I fired about ten shots with the Lee-Enfield .303 rifle. I was reasonably good with a rifle, having done lots of rabbit shooting on my uncle's property with a .22 rifle. Although the .303 was an entirely different type of rifle to use, I did pretty well, and there was a group of us picked out by an officer who had come to visit the Showground from the 2/30th Battalion. That afternoon we were told we were to go to Bathurst the next morning to join the 2/30th Battalion.

I'll never forget arriving at Bathurst. We were welcomed by the adjutant and then taken to another building to meet our CO, the man we came to know as Black Jack Galleghan.

He asked us what training we had. We told him we had been at the Showground for six months, and I remember his words very well. 'Okay then . . . right. Your training starts from now,' he said. 'Forget what you learned down there, you're going to start all over again.' A groan went up. We thought of all those long days at the Showground on various military tactics, including bayonet practice and running up hills and jumping over walls and wading through little streams around in Centennial Park. That was pretty rough, but it was a kindergarten compared with the training we had with the 2/30th. You see, the battalion had been formed for about eight months at that time and we had some catching up to do.

In July 1941, we were given a piece of paper with the words 'FINAL LEAVE' written across it. It also served as a railway ticket, and my destination was Matong. During my final seven days' leave with my uncle and cousins, we went to Wagga for the day. One of my cousins, Frank Quinn, had also joined the army and he was in camp in Victoria. He was home on leave too, and while we were walking down in Wagga I looked in the window of a camera shop.

My uncle said 'Would you like a camera?' And I said 'Oh, yes, Uncle Jack.' He said 'Okay, we'll go in and pick one out.' Then he said to his son Frank, 'Well, you might as well have one too, because it won't be long before you'll be going away I suppose.'

We went in and picked out two identical cameras. They were the first of the folding type Kodak 2 Brownie cameras with a 6.2 lens. I think they cost about £3 each. The folding camera was a fairly new idea with Kodak, an updated version of the box Brownie. My uncle bought them for us and the chap in the photographic shop showed us how to put a film in.

My uncle had some business to attend to with a stock and station agent and he told us to amuse ourselves. So we walked around Wagga taking photographs and familiarising ourselves with the cameras. I took various photos with mine, just aiming at whatever I thought would be a good photo, pressing the release, and hoping everything would turn out all right. I still have some of the photos I took that day.

Back on my uncle's property I took more photos – one of my pony, the horse I used to ride. He was the one I used when I joined the 21st Light Horse. I also took a couple of shots of ten-horse teams pulling an implement called a combine. It was actually planting wheat, which is done in the colder weather.

Looking back on those times, I was pleased to have the camera but I didn't have any specific feelings about it. It formed part of

Fordson tractor, Matong

my kit, the same way as my razor and shaving brush. It wasn't until we actually got to Singapore and Malaya, to a different country, climate, people and totally different ways of life, that I really got keen about using it.

I do remember taking photos of some of the chaps in a troop train when we boarded the train at Kelso just out of Bathurst. Most of the 27th Brigade went out by train on that morning.

We embarked on a Dutch ship, the *Johann van Oldenbarneveld*. I did take photos of some of our blokes playing tunnel ball and other sporting activities on board. There is a shot of our CO Black

(Above and below) Barracks huts, Bathurst, July, 1941

Jack Galleghan, with some of his staff, and I photographed one of our navy escort vessels during the voyage to Fremantle and on to Singapore.

We landed at Collier Quay in Singapore, and the first thing that struck us was the heat and the smells. There was a monsoon rain squall on the afternoon we arrived and we disembarked in a heavy downpour. We stood beside the ship like half-drowned rats, waiting and wondering what was going to happen to us next. It was all very bewildering. Many of us were only virtually overgrown boys at the time. You see we didn't even know we were going to Singapore until we were a couple of days out of Sydney. We had thought we were going to the Middle East.

Singapore was such a totally different environment to Australia that it was the thing to do to race around taking photos of everything you thought was of interest to send back home. I was one of the ones that did a lot of this and I sent the photos home to my mother – and that is why I still have some of them. Everything was fascinating, the different views of buildings and streets, the rickshaws, roadside food stalls, Chinese junks and barges, and the tropical surroundings.

We had five weeks in Singapore, quartered at Birdwood Camp. I had become a keen photographer during that time, but I didn't know much about processing photographs. I got to know a Chinese photographer called Wong Yeow, who had a photographic shop in Changi Village. Some of my mates used to get me to take their films down for processing and printing so they could send them home.

One night I said to him, 'Can you do this one very quickly, my friends want to catch the mail home?' So he said, 'Oh yes, come in to my darkroom and I'll show you how they're done.' He was

Troop ship *Aquitania* through porthole of the *Johann Van Olden-Barneveldt*
This was taken just outside Sydney Heads travelling down the New South Wales coast.

View of Fremantle docks

Naval escort off Fremantle

I took this photo on the first day out from Fremantle heading for Singapore. There is some doubt about its identification, but it could be HMAS *Perth*.

Morning exercises on board troopship

The substantial figure of our CO Black Jack Galleghan (back to camera, right) watching D Company playing tunnel ball.

Our leaders in tropical gear
Entering the tropics, and a change of uniform. From left, Captain Ward Booth, Lieutenant Colonel
Fred Galleghan, and our adjutant, Lieutenant Stuart Peach.

an amiable bloke in his mid-forties and he taught me quite a bit
about processing film and printing it. I used to spend about two
nights a week there for the first five weeks we were in Singapore.
I would go down to Changi Village after working hours and stay
with him from 6 pm until about 10 or 11 pm. The main job was
to help with the various stages of processing, particularly of films
taken by blokes in my unit. I used to collect all the films and take
them to be processed and printed. This was good business for
Wong, and at the same time I was learning something that stood
me in good stead later on.

Canal scene, Malacca

Malay fishing village near Malacca

General view, Singapore river

Transport, Malayan style, Batu Pahat

Malay mosque, Batu Pahat

Yak cart with banana leaves, Malacca

Mobile food vendor, near Batu Pahat

Looking out towards the Straits of Malacca

I used to look forward to going down to Changi Village to see Wong. He would call out to his wife, who would bring us cups of tea. He spoke very good English, and we used to have lots of conversations about Australia and China. He had left mainland China when he was a small boy. He told me about his schooling in China, and stories his mother had told him about China. I remember he used to talk a lot about the Japanese and the Chinese attitude towards them. He used to say, 'If the Japanese come here, you must be very careful. They are very bad people.' Apparently he knew a lot about what the Japanese were doing in China at that time. We became quite good friends.

Actually my visits to see Wong Yeow and his family got me my nickname, 'Changi' Aspinall. I was often down at his shop in the village until quite late at night processing photographs, way past the time we were supposed to be back in barracks for bed check at 8 pm. A friend of mine, the corporal who was in charge of the hut I was in, would say, 'Oh, he's down at Changi.' And it sort of stuck, and I became 'Changi' Aspinall. Some of my friends still call me that.

After five weeks at Birdwood Camp in Singapore, the battalion moved to Batu Pahat, about sixty miles north of Singapore Island, on the west coast of Malaya. Our camp was just on the outskirts of the town and we spent a lot of time there, getting to know various people. There was a special canteen set up for us by some of the European women in the area. It was an entertainment centre where you could write letters, have a cup of tea and cake, and enjoy the various comforts such as the Red Cross would supply in Australia.

I became very keen on photography at this stage. Having had some agricultural background, I was intrigued by the water buffaloes.

The Malays used them not only as beasts of burden, but to pull single-furrow ploughs in the paddy fields. The paddy fields were under water and the ploughs looked very antiquated pieces of equipment, and that fascinated me. Also the type of houses they lived in, which were mainly built of thatched leaves called *atap*. They were built on stilts high up off the ground. There were fishing villages, where their whole livelihood circulated around the fish they caught and the boats they went out in. They made their own nets, and I found all this extremely interesting.

Of course our military training had to start all over again. The training we had at Bathurst was more or less patterned on desert warfare. Now we had to learn jungle tactics in a hurry. We would march out along the roads in single file, a platoon on each side of the road. An area would be chosen – usually a combination of a rubber estate, with some open going and some rough jungle. We would be given a certain position to take and we learned to camouflage ourselves and move silently through the jungle. Concealment and stealth were the objects of our training at the time. Sometimes our CO Black Jack Galleghan would come and watch us on these stunts, as we used to call them. If he wasn't satisfied, he gave the officers and NCOs a bit of a blast the next day that would be handed down to us and we would perform in the way we were required to.

Although we took our training seriously, there was a feeling that we were on a sort of holiday. We didn't know if we were going to stay in Malaya. There was talk that we might go to the Middle East. We thought we were in Malaya in case the Germans sent an occupation force to try and take Malaya. We didn't really think much about Japan.

Changing the guard, Birdwood camp

Meanwhile, we enjoyed ourselves as much as we could in the little town of Batu Pahat. A lot of the blokes were very keen on photography, and several photographic studios sprang up in the town when it was realised there was some money to be made from the troops in the area. One of the better studios was run by a man called Mah Lee. Troops used to go down to his studio to have their photograph taken, and he used to visit our camp to take group shots, such as company and platoon photos. One particular one I remember is of my Transport Platoon sitting and standing in front of their vehicles. I bought a copy from Mah Lee and sent it home to my mother.

Atap huts, Batu Pahat camp, Malaya

We slept in these huts on Indian-style charpoy beds.

What we didn't know was that Mah Lee was not Chinese, but Japanese! If the technology had been available, I'm sure the pictures he was taking in our military area would have been flashed to Tokyo by the next morning. As it was, he was always finding excuses to get into the camp – either with his big half-plate camera, or his shoulder 35 mm camera – to take pictures. I'd say he probably knew more about our camp at Batu Pahat than we did. I'm sure his pictures did get back to Tokyo in some way, because the camp area was heavily bombed later on, although the British were in the area at that time, not us.

Brewster Buffalo aircraft at Kluang airfield, Malaya

One of Mah Lee's photographs that I still have was taken after a dinner at the Batu Pahat Chinese Chamber of Commerce. This photo included officers and NCOs of the 2/30th Battalion, and the Chinese businessmen who had entertained us. We know now that this photograph was used by the Japanese to identify and execute most of the Chinese businessmen who were in it. One of the Chinese who survived told me in later years that he was tipped off about what was happening to his friends and he escaped from Batu Pahat to Sabah in Borneo to avoid being killed.

Not long after we became prisoners of war, some of our unit were working on a shrine the Japanese were building on top of Bukit

Group of D Company, Batu Pahat

(*Back row l to r*) Norm Lee, George Choat, Wal Barnes, Brian (Blue) Woods, AR (Jerry) Cox, (Unknown), Len Barnes, George Aspinall

(*Front row l to r*) Norm Grist, Tom Gardiner, Jim Baird, Bill Fletcher, Alf Carroll

Timah Hill, in Singapore. A bloke called Kevin Ward came up to me during a smoko and said, 'You'll never guess who the interpreter is on this job . . . it's Mah Lee, the photographer from Batu Pahat!' I kept well away from him, because I had had a few cross words with him one day when he overcharged me for some prints. But there was no doubt it was Mah Lee. He was wearing a captain's uniform complete with a great big sword, and he was particularly unfriendly towards us. He made the guards put us on the dirtiest

Mess hut, Batu Pahat

jobs. Apparently he claimed that some of our blokes hadn't paid for the photographic work he had done for them!

So Mah Lee had been a very successful spy. We never saw him again, apart from that one occasion. Perhaps it was just as well. But it showed how good the Japanese intelligence was and how well prepared they were when they did land in Malaya.

Of course we were blissfully unaware of this at Batu Pahat from August to December 1941. On the night of 8 December 1941, we were having a concert in our mess hut when the show was interrupted by Lieutenant Colonel Galleghan, who said that Japan had entered

2/30th Transport Platoon, Batu Pahat

This is one of the photographs taken by the Japanese spy, Mah Lee, in our camp at Batu Pahat. I am sitting third from the left, second row.

the war and an invasion of Malaya was imminent. We were told to go and get our sleep, and we would be moving out early in the morning to take up battle stations. Next morning everybody packed up all their gear. Anything surplus you couldn't get into a haversack had to be put in a kitbag and left at the quartermaster's store. My pack included a groundsheet, a couple of changes of clothes and some personal items – including my camera. At 10 am we moved out of our camp at Batu Pahat to the aerodrome at Kluang. The rifle companies formed up in different positions around the 'drome

Officers and NCOs outside Chinese Chamber of Commerce, Batu Pahat

This photograph was also taken by Mah Lee, and later used to identify and execute many of the Asian businessmen pictured.

and some of our vehicles were driven on to the runway to block any enemy aircraft that might come in. They were shifted when the RAF wanted to use the 'drome.

We left Kluang shortly after that and went to a position along the road between Mersing and Jemaluang on the east coast of Malaya. We had to camouflage all our vehicles off the road in the jungle, and we were there for several days. News reached us that the Japanese had landed at Kota Bharu, but we didn't know any details. All we knew was that they had landed in northern Malaya and we

Battle station bivouac, Jemaluang Road, Mersing

were taking up positions in case they tried to land at Mersing. After about a week at Jemaluang, word came through that the battalion was to move to the Segamat–Gemas area.

At that particular stage my company commander told me I wouldn't be going up with the battalion, that I had to go to a medical unit, the 2/4th Casualty Clearing Station just outside Segamat. When the different units went into action, the wounded came back through us and I had to collect their equipment, rifles, ammunition and grenades, disarm it all and store it in the truck – which was kept well away from the casualty clearing station. When I had enough equipment, I had to take it back to Johor Bahru and deliver it to base headquarters.

When the 2/30th went into action just north of Gemas, I had been allocated back from the Gemas area. The ambulances weren't allowed to go closer than a road about three or four miles away from the action, so the wounded were carried to us by stretcher. We would take the wounded from the casualty clearing stations to the nearest hospital, which at that time was at Johor Bahru. On several occasions while I was bringing wounded back, Japanese aircraft could be seen approaching. I had a medical orderly on the ambulance who used to act as a spotter. He'd give the alarm, and we'd all dive out of the ambulance into the nearest drain on the side of the road. The Japs used to delight in shooting up any vehicles that were on a road, whether they had red crosses marked on them or not. On two occasions, I ran the ambulance right off the road and ended up in a ditch to get out of their way. I'd heard the machine-gun fire from the aircraft on several occasions and it really put the wind up me. I didn't like it at all. We did whatever we could for people in vehicles who were hit by these aircraft. On one occasion, a couple of chaps in the back of my ambulance were hit and the medical orderly attended to them on the run.

We had been told all sorts of nonsense about the Japanese soldiers, how they could hardly see and how they didn't fight at night and a lot of other rubbish. We soon developed a healthy respect for their fighting abilities. For one thing, they didn't seem to need a lot of motor transport, as they often broke down their field guns into components and carried them by hand. This made them very self-contained when it came to moving through the jungle. One of their most effective tactics was never to try a frontal assault. They had a knack of getting behind people. If there was a group of them, they'd break up and make a fork – one section of their troops would go around to the left, and the other section around to the right. And they had a nasty little habit of using firecrackers. You'd hear these crackers go off on the left and then on the right. Perhaps they were a scare tactic or a signalling device. But not long after you'd hear the crackers go off, the two groups would appear to attack us from the rear. Quite often they had us virtually surrounded, and then it was a tough hand-to-hand battle to get out of that situation. A lot of our chaps got out of these situations and killed quite a few Japanese while they were doing so. But this seemed to me their most effective and persistent tactic.

Eventually all the different defence forces, English, Australian and Indian, were pushed off the mainland of Malaya back to Singapore Island. I was still driving ambulances or trucks, carrying the surplus equipment of the wounded who were in the hospitals. There was a strict rule that all casualty clearing stations and hospitals had to be kept free of any arms or ammunition. I had to collect all weapons from the wounded and make sure they surrendered them. I understood then this was part of the Geneva Convention, that there were to be no weapons within the confines of a Red Cross flag. We stuck pretty rigidly to that, although when I thought of some of the massacres that took place later, there wasn't much point to it. But that was the job I was given to do and I tried to do it.

I preferred to be on the ambulances, which led into some quite hectic situations. It was virtually a twenty-four hour a day job. I'd just try and snatch some sleep in the driver's seat between journeys. I'd try to park the ambulance under a tree or somewhere invisible

Ambulances in the grounds of St Andrew's Cathedral – Singapore
I took this photograph on the morning after the surrender, while we were waiting for the Japanese to arrive. St Andrew's Cathedral had been used as a hospital in the final stages of the battle for Singapore.

to aircraft because they had no respect for Red Cross markings, or for any markings at all. If a vehicle was out in the open, it would be fired on from the air. Towards the end, I was picking up civilians who had been injured by bombing or shelling and bringing them in to casualty stations like the Cathay Building or St Andrew's Cathedral. On the morning of the surrender, 15 February 1942, I had just brought back six wounded people from the Tanglin area of Singapore when I was told that the surrender had been signed and we were to cease all activities forthwith.

Bombed vehicles in the grounds of St Andrew's Cathedral

It never crossed my mind that we would surrender. I was amazed. And so were all the other troops I spoke to. It was always understood that we would fight to the very end if necessary. But as we know now, the surrender was necessary to save the civilian population. The Japanese were carrying out a technique of block bombing. They would pick out a certain residential area and literally blow it to pieces. The other factor was the water situation. They had control of the water on Singapore and it had been cut off. A lot of us weren't aware of these things when the surrender took place.

It was an unreal time, just like a bad dream. It was so bewildering that we just carried on normally. It wasn't as though we stood out on the road and put our hands up in the air, nothing like that. We just stayed at our different posts. A lot of our people were still armed to act as police, to prevent looting or general disorder. It was not till late in the afternoon of that first day that some Japanese patrols came into Singapore.

During this unreal period, after the surrender but before the Japanese had taken over, I decided to take some photographs. A couple of bombs had landed on St Andrew's Cathedral and there were a number of burnt-out ambulances and utility trucks in the cathedral grounds. I photographed some of those and then took a walk along the waterfront at about 9 am and took a photo looking back towards the General Post Office. There were great clouds of smoke rising up in the distance from the oil tanks at Bukit Timah, or somewhere in that direction. And that was the last photo I took before I became a prisoner of the Japanese.

'OH, GEE – I'VE STILL GOT ME CAMERA'

I'd driven my ambulance out of the St Andrew's Cathedral grounds and parked it beside the road. I was standing at the front of it, leaning on the bonnet, when a group of Japanese soldiers rode by on bicycles. They just gave me a bit of a look, nothing that I could make any sense of. I was expecting one of them to come and say something to me, like what was I doing there with the ambulance. But they just rode past and had a casual look, and that was my first close-up experience with the Japanese as a prisoner of war.

A general order went out all over the island that all surrendered Allied troops were to assemble and march out to the Changi area, to Selarang Barracks. I was with a medical section and we assembled near St Andrew's Cathedral. There were ten Japanese soldiers lined up on the opposite side of the road, and with a lot of sign language, grunts, moans and shouts of *kurrah* (come here!) they indicated we were to pick up what gear we had and start marching down the road towards Changi.

114

Bomb-damaged civilian houses, Changi Peninsula

Some POWs were quartered in bomb-damaged civilian houses near Selarang. This photograph was taken from the Selarang water tower and the Roberts Barracks water tower can be seen in the distance silhouetted against the Straits of Johor.

If you had an aerial view, you would have seen a long line of Allied troops marching towards Changi from various parts of the island during the next three days. Those who couldn't walk were taken by our ambulances that were still in operation. I will never forget that march. The local people were all lined up beside the road watching us walk past. The Chinese were particularly sympathetic, offering us bananas, coconuts and drinks of water when they could. I think they were as bewildered as we were that we had suddenly become prisoners of war.

Just about every house on the road had a little Japanese flag out in front of it. We often wondered about this. I don't know about the Malays, but I am sure the Chinese did not fly those flags. It was probably done by the Japanese for propaganda purposes because there were photographers and film groups covering our progress to Changi.

I think we were all still in a kind of shock. My thoughts didn't go beyond the immediate situation. We just concentrated on marching where we had to go. There was no thought to the future.

The Japanese had decided to put all the Allied prisoners of war on the Changi Peninsula on the east side of Singapore Island. Although Changi Gaol was in that area, we didn't go there until much later – until after we had been to the Thai–Burma Railway in fact. A lot of people think we were in Changi Gaol all the time, but that wasn't so. At first there wasn't even any barbed wire. We just congregated in and around the buildings of the Selarang Barracks. After all, there was nowhere to escape to and the Japanese knew this. They adopted the policy very early of letting us look after ourselves.

When we first arrived at Selarang, we were lined up for several hours, waiting for the next move. Then we were assigned our particular billets. I was reassigned from the 2/10th Field Ambulance back to my own 2/30th Battalion. I reported to my CO, Lieutenant Colonel Galleghan, and was allocated a space about six or seven feet long by about three or four feet wide on the concrete floor of one of the barracks buildings. And that's where I slept, among quite a few hundred other troops. Throughout the day we sort of milled about looking for mates that we hadn't seen for some time, and talking about what might happen to us. This went on for some weeks. We were virtually doing nothing at that stage.

Indian Sikh guards' quarters

Most of the Indian Sikh troops went over to the Japanese and were given the job of guarding us. I took this shot of some of their quarters from the British POW camp at Roberts Barracks.

Selarang Barracks was the main camp for the Australians. There were English and Dutch troops on other parts of the Changi Peninsula. We had some Dutch in our area and Roberts Barracks nearby was the hospital, and where the bulk of the British troops were congregated.

Not long after we arrived in Changi I was going through my haversack and I thought, 'Oh, gee – I've still got me camera!' And

The guards' quarters
A closer look at one of the Sikh guards' huts on the road between Selarang and Roberts Barracks. We hated the Sikhs because they were not only traitors in our eyes, but they used to beat us up whenever they got the opportunity.

I had about five or six 620 films. There were eight exposures on a 620 film. They had a black paper backing on them and they were wound onto a spool. The size of each negative was 3¼ inches by 2¼ inches.

I started thinking about the camera and what I ought to do with it – whether I should break it up and throw it away. But anyway, I loaded one of the films into the camera and started to take some photographs around the Selarang area. It was quite open at that time and there were no Jap guards inside the perimeter so there wasn't much risk. I made a point of not letting people in our own administration know what I was doing as well. The officers thought I'd be endangering the rest of the troops. I didn't think so at the time and I don't think anyone else did. I think the fact that nobody else had a camera might have upset them a bit. My only thoughts at the time were that there was an opportunity to get photos of an unusual situation. I didn't have any great design in mind for making a documentary record or anything like that. It was just something to keep my mind occupied more than anything. I thought it would be good to get the photos back to Australia and perhaps show them to my mother or relations or anybody that was interested. They were just general photos, as I'd been taking earlier of my trip to Malaya. I suppose it was my photographic diary.

During these early days at Selarang Barracks I found I could take photographs without much risk. The Japanese left us to look after ourselves, within our area on the Changi Peninsula. I climbed up a very prominent water tower next to the barracks and took some general views of the area.

One clearly shows the garden area we were cultivating to try and supplement the eternal diet of rice. You can see a group of POWs working on the sweet potatoes and other tropical vegetables we tried to grow. We used to boil the leaves of the tapioca and sweet potato plants to get vitamin B. The palm trees were good value too. Troops were forbidden to pick the coconuts, and they were harvested at various times and made up into a milky substance. This mulched-up coconut juice and a bit of water was given to sick men as a diet supplement. We had some Queenslanders who were experts at climbing palm trees. They made a hook device that used to fit on their feet, and they would shin up the trees easily just as they did back home.

I also got some pictures of our living quarters at Selarang. It rained quite a lot and we had to hang up our clothes inside to

Birdwood Camp, Changi Peninsula
Another shot from the water tower, looking slightly to the right of the bomb-damaged houses, showing Birdwood Camp. This was our first barracks when we arrived in Singapore in August 1941.

dry. We had makeshift beds about three feet apart. They were called *charpoys* and consisted of a rope net made from coconut husks used as a mattress, suspended from a four-post frame. You can also see things like water bottles, kit bags, makeshift chairs and various bits and pieces we had collected. A lot of us still had some equipment and clothing we had carried to Changi in the first place.

Quite a lot of these early shots show our blokes eating rice. In the early days, when we still had some tins of bully beef, the cooks

General view, Changi Peninsula
Another shot from the Selarang water tower. Part of Birdwood Camp can be seen in the background.

used to make up a kind of rice and bully beef hash. That wasn't too bad. But it wasn't long before we were eating only rice, and whatever green vegetables or anything that could be mixed with it. But mostly it was just rice.

I never liked rice, although I ate virtually nothing else for three-and-a-half years. During the time we were trying to get used to the new rice diet, I took quite a few photographs of men in our unit in Selarang, sitting down eating their issue of rice. You can see that most of us are still reasonably well dressed. Being so early

Vegetable garden at Selarang
We were allowed to supplement our rice diet by growing vegetables like sweet potatoes and tapioca. The leaves of the tapioca root were boiled to get vitamin B. Some of our fellows can be seen under one of the coconut palms.

in the period of captivity, our clothes had not deteriorated to any great extent.

Later on, our cooks became very good rice cooks, but at first they had no idea. I suppose the only rice they had experienced in Australia was in rice puddings. And that's how the rice was presented, in a kind of gluey soup. Actually it wasn't all the cooks' fault. The rice we were issued with came from a bombed godown on the Singapore docks. It was what we knew as 'broken rice', and it had been mixed with lime – probably to keep the weevils out of it. It had a most unpleasant taste and was very gritty. Sometimes the outsides of the grains were soft, but the inside was as hard as shell-grit. It was a bit rough on the men with crook teeth. If you were served from the top of the rice bucket, it was fairly dry. But near the bottom it was a kind of rice slop.

Our doctors were worried that we weren't getting enough vitamins, so working parties were sent out to gather great bundles of *lalang* grass. In the early days, bundles of this grass were put into 44-gallon drums and boiled over a fire for many hours. It was thought that this would be a source of vitamin B. Later on, the grass was minced up in a kind of coffee-grinder type of contraption

Eating rice, Selarang

A sit-down dinner. Unfortunately the emulsion on this negative has lifted but I can identify Harry Riches (bald head and moustache) and a chap named Bruce Campbell on his right. Wilf Evans can be seen on the extreme right-hand side of the photo.

Serving rice

As well as your pint of rice, you got half a pint of grass soup. This tasted absolutely awful, and was made from boiled lalang grass. It was supposed to give us vitamins, but some of us couldn't face it.

Eating rice

Another water-damaged negative. Arthur Isaac is on the extreme right of this shot and Tommy Lee is spooning up some rice in the centre of the group. Tommy was lost on the Thai–Burma Railway.

Cooking rice, Mount Pleasant

We boiled our rice in 44-gallon drums, and then carried containers of it to the various houses we were quartered in at that time. Jack Black has his back to the camera.

Serving rice

I took this from the balcony of the house we were living in during our time at Mount Pleasant. Two of our blokes are diving down into the bucket for the last of the rice.

that was built up from various bits and pieces of machinery about the place. The finished brew was called grass soup, and you were supposed to drink half a pint of this foul stuff with your pint of rice. A lot of the men had become very constipated on the plain rice diet and some had not had a bowel movement for ten or eleven days. Well, the grass soup certainly fixed that, but it tasted so awful a lot of us wouldn't drink it.

What made the rice taste even worse was that we had no salt to add to it. Working parties were organised to carry salt water up from Changi Beach to cook the rice in, to make it a bit more palatable. I used to go on some of these salt water parties, and on occasions I would take my camera with me. On the way down to the beach, we would go past some of the huge 15-inch gun emplacements that had been blown up the night before the surrender to the Japanese. There were no Jap guards with us, only our own NCOs, and we would stop and have a good look at the guns. I took several photos. In one you can see the people in the water-carrying party standing beside it which gives an indication of how huge they were. I was just interested in getting everyday snapshots of our life during the early days at Selarang.

For the first two or three weeks at Selarang we were virtually left to our own resources. Black Jack Galleghan was tougher than some of the other commanders. He had us on the parade grounds marching around and doing exercises. His idea was to keep us physically fit so that we would still be a fighting force, in the event of an Allied landing or some such occurrence. But it wasn't long before the Japanese decided to make use of all this energy and manpower, and the Allied units were told they had to supply as many fit men

Wrecked 15-inch gun, Changi

Not long after I took this picture, these guns were cut up and sent back to Japan as scrap metal, as the barrels contained a large amount of copper.

as were needed to go in to Singapore on what we called working parties. The particular group that I was with was quartered in a place called the Great World. It was an entertainment centre, rather like Sydney's Luna Park.

We were formed into gangs of 100 to 150 men and my group was assigned to the Singapore dock area. The huge storage sheds there were called godowns, and they were crammed full of almost anything you could name. Our job was to load all this cargo into ships, which would take it to Japan. There were raw materials like rubber. There were cars and trucks in crates that had never been unpacked. There were even several brand-new aircraft all crated up, sitting on the docks. We had to shift the cargo so that cranes

We were allowed to go to Changi beach to cart salt water back to cook our rice in, and I took my camera one day and photographed one of the huge 15-inch guns that were blown up by the British shortly before the surrender.

could lift it up into the holds of the waiting ships. This went on for two or three weeks, and we were moved to another area – which was a great improvement. We called it 'Nestlé House' where Nestlé products like condensed milk and chocolate were stored. We helped ourselves to as much as we could!

Food was very much on our minds. We hadn't become accustomed to the rice-based diet, and we were prepared to take risks to scrounge anything that was edible or usable from the dock area and smuggle it back to camp, either for ourselves or for our mates. We had all sorts of ways of doing this. We stashed stuff under our hats or stuffed it down our shirts, if we had a shirt, and somehow got it back to the Great World. Everybody smoked in those days,

You can get an idea of the enormous size of these guns by some of the water-carrying party standing at the left of the tilted traversing platform. It was said these guns could only fire out to sea, but this one was modified to turn inland towards the advancing Japanese.

and next to Nestlé House was a big depot for Wills cigarettes and cigars. Now that was a real gold mine because we were running short of tobacco and we'd been smoking all sorts of rubbish like Java weed, which tastes as though it is made from seaweed. The first few puffs went right through the top of your head. When we had to shift big wooden crates of cigarettes, some always seemed to slip off the slide we were using, and crash on to the ground, and cartons of cigarettes were scattered around. Not all of these found their way back into the original container, so we had plenty of tobacco at that time, and a lot of it got back to camp. The Japanese used to have searches in the late afternoon but they weren't too serious about it in those days. All they did was tap you on the shoulders

Japanese guarding 6-inch gun, Singapore docks

This is probably one of my most risky shots, taken through a hole in a warehouse wall of a Japanese soldier guarding a 6-inch gun. He *seems* to be looking straight at the camera!

and down the body and between the legs with a wooden baton. If they didn't find anything, they'd go on to the next bloke. When we worked out how they were searching that day, we'd make sure we hid our loot somewhere else.

They didn't wake up for a long time that you could get quite a number of cigarettes into the sweat band inside your slouch hat. We managed to get a lot of stuff out in our hats.

This went on for quite some time. Then one day a Japanese lieutenant – he wasn't a bad bloke really, but he knew just enough English to get himself into bother – lined us up for the routine search. But instead he gave us a little speech. The gist of it was that he knew how we were knocking stuff off and he was going to demonstrate how we did it. First he got a tin of condensed milk and put it down on the ground. Then he took a slouch hat and, sidling up to the tin with great pretending cunning, he dropped it over the tin. Then he jumped up onto a crate to address us.

'Now you Australian soldier,' he said, 'I am going to speak to you in your own language.'

'You think we Japanese stupid people, that Japanese soldier not know what Australian soldier steal. You think we know fuck nothing what happens here.

'Well you are wrong, Australian soldier. We Japanese know fuck-all!'

Then he picked up the slouch hat to show us the tin of condensed milk he had hidden. But the tin had gone. One of our blokes had knocked it off while he was giving his little speech!

Well he jumped and ranted and raved and carried on and got some of his guards to really start searching. Up to this point, some of the guards weren't too bad. If you had a packet of cigarettes, they might let you keep them. Of course if you had a couple of cartons, they'd give you a bit of a bashing and take them off you.

But this time everything was confiscated, whether it came from the docks or not. It was all put in a heap and taken away. Things got much tougher after that. But I still think it was worth it. A sense of humour was as good as a pint of rice. Once you lost your sense of humour – which some other nationalities did – you were in a bad way.

From then on, if any loot was found on anyone, the Japs would line us all up and half a dozen of them would come along the line giving everyone a bashing, no matter whether they had stolen anything or not. But we were desperate to get extra food, as we found it hard to acclimatise to eating rice. The method we finished up with was not to be too greedy and to just try to get away with say one packet of cigarettes, or a tin of sardines. Someone else might score a jar of Vegemite (the Japs thought it was boot polish) and in that way we got a bit of extra food back to the Great World. But, like everything else, one packet of cigarettes became two, then three, and the Japanese would wake up to the racket, and they would crack down again. There were threats of being shot if anyone was caught stealing from the docks. I don't know if anybody was ever shot for that reason, but quite a lot got severe bashings with sticks, or rifle butts, or jabs in the backside with bayonets. But, looking back, these were the good times. We had plenty of food and the Japanese soldiers looking after us were front-line troops. Many of them didn't care too much about looking after prisoners. Not long after, they were moved on to New Guinea or some other war area and the occupation forces replaced them. They were mostly poor types and much more brutal, particularly the Koreans.

Occasionally I'd carry my camera with me if I thought I could get a good shot. I had a policy of not taking pictures of the Japanese, in case they caught up with me, but I was rather intrigued by a 6-inch naval gun down on the docks that always had a Jap guard beside it. It was a bit cheeky, I suppose, but one day I smuggled my camera into one of the godowns opposite this gun and took a shot through a hole in the galvanised iron wall. When you look at the photo, the guard appears to be looking straight at the camera. But he had no idea he was being photographed.

By this time I had worked out a pretty safe way of carrying the camera. Being a folding model, it was fairly flat – about five inches long, three inches wide and about an inch and a half thick. To take a picture you had to open up the front of the camera and pull out a bellows which gave you sufficient depth of focus. I noticed that a lot of the Japanese wore a kidney belt, a bit like a scaled down version of those sashes worn by Sumo wrestlers. I fashioned a thick canvas kidney belt, with one important difference. It had an inner pocket which could be closed with a couple of press studs. I used to carry the camera in that, snuggled into the small of my back. If I had a shirt on, I'd let that fall over it. It wouldn't have survived a really thorough search but, thank goodness, that never happened while I was actually carrying the camera.

PROCESSING AND PRINTING

ALL MY EARLY PHOTOGRAPHS IN SELARANG, AND DOWN ON THE DOCKS, WERE TAKEN WITH THE few rolls of 620 film I had with me in my haversack when I marched into Changi. I started to think how I was going to get them processed, because I knew enough about the effect of tropical climate on unprocessed film to know that they would soon be ruined. The hot sticky climate over there caused photographic material to deteriorate very quickly. I even thought it might be possible to get out of camp one night and take them somewhere to be processed – but I didn't think too much of that idea! I kept the exposed films hidden in one of the buildings we were living in while I thought what I might do. I wasn't greatly concerned about them at that stage because I only had five or six rolls of film, and once they were finished, that would be that.

Then one day on the Singapore docks I chanced on a lot of X-ray photographic equipment in one of the godowns. I noticed that there were boxes of negative film, bottles of developer and various chemicals just lying about, and the Japanese didn't seem to be particularly interested in it. I thought about it for a while and it sort of grew on me. I knew I was running out of 620 film and I wondered whether some of the X-ray film would be suitable to use in my camera. I had learned a bit about photography and general processing while I had helped Wong Yeow in his darkroom in my first weeks in Singapore. Anyway, I thought I'd try to get a box of that X-ray film – it was in sheets of various sizes – and do some experimenting.

I picked up a box of X-ray negative sheets about ten inches by eight inches which was still sealed, and shoved it down the front of my shorts. I managed to conceal it with my shirt hanging over the front of it and smuggled it back to the Great World where we were bivouacked. I thought if I could cut up a strip of this material into the right size to fit in the back of my camera, I would try and take a photograph with it.

But first I had to find a way of processing negatives. Back in the godown I had seen plenty of X-ray developer – crates of it in fact. I knew that X-ray material tends to produce a coarser grain in film and I thought this might be a problem. Anyway, I got one of these big jars of X-ray developer and decanted some into a Tiger beer bottle, sealed it with a rubber cork, and managed to get it back to camp. The next day I started hunting for some hypo (fixing solution). It's all very well having developer, but if you can't stop the developing process with another chemical, it just keeps on going and you finish up with no image at all. Not all the bottles were labelled, but I knew what hypo smelt like because of my experience working with Wong Yeow in his darkroom. In fact once you smell hypo it's difficult to forget. After sniffing a lot of different jars and

Harry Russell underneath a bore-hole auger tripod, Selarang
Harry is sitting on the shaft of the auger, with the welded shovels on the head visible on the right.

bottles I found one that smelt like the ingredient I was looking for. If must have been, because it did the job!

My first experiment was to see if the X-ray film would work at all. I found a dark corner under a flight of stairs in one of the buildings at the Great World. This became my first darkroom. I had some old photographs and my idea was to use one of them to see if I could transfer the image onto a piece of X-ray material by shining a light through under a glass plate. I did not have high hopes of the result, but I thought there wouldn't be much

The Roman Catholic chapel, Selarang
This little chapel was built by the POWs, supervised by the padres. The altar end was under cover, and the seats were out in the open. The pictures on the wall were painted by some of the men.

point in cutting up the X-ray film to fit my camera if the negative material would not hold an image. I knew my camera was a fairly cheap one and not capable of producing photographs with very high definition.

The container I took the developer from had instructions that it was to be broken down to ten parts of water to one part of raw developer. I found a little enamelled kidney dish, which had probably come from a hospital, for the developing solution. I sawed a coconut in half, and used the bottom half without the eyes in it for the hypo – but it rocked around too much, and I eventually changed to a split section of bamboo. However it did the job for the first experiment, which was carried out in the little hideaway I found under a stairway. I had a battery and a globe, and I found a bit of red bunting lying around the Great World, which had been an amusement park as I think I mentioned. I wrapped the bunting around the globe, and this made a red glow – just enough for me to see what I was doing.

I hadn't worked out proper developing times at that stage, but when I finished I could see I had a blurred image on the piece of X-ray negative that had been used in the experiment with the old photograph and the glass plate. That was very pleasing, because I knew that I could not only go on taking photographs, but develop them as well. I had virtually an unlimited supply of negatives, and plenty of chemicals to process them with.

The next job was to see how I could adapt the outsize sheets of 10-inch by 8-inch sheets of X-ray negative to fit my Kodak 2 camera. Working at night in my little darkroom under the stairs, I measured the width between the spools of my 620 film, and cut some of the bigger X-ray negative sheets into strips, which gave me four exposures 2¼ inches by 3¼ inches. I took some of the black paper from the films I had already used and rolled the X-ray strips back into it.

But I did not have nearly enough spools, so I had to work out a method to enable me to use individual sections of film in the camera – in other words, one shot at a time. In the daylight, I opened up my camera and made a template with a piece of cardboard of the actual dimensions of the piece of film I would later cut down to fit

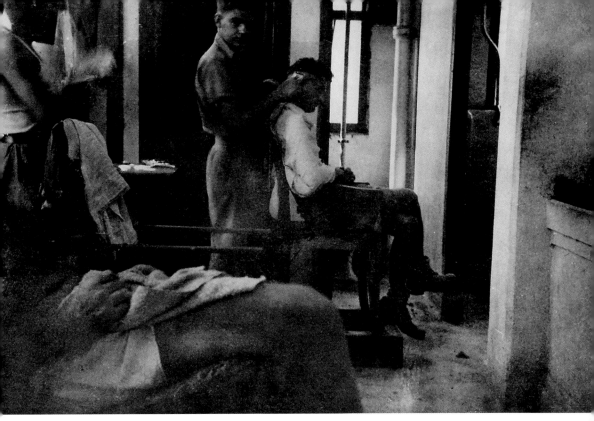

Darby Young's barber shop, Selarang

Darby never had clippers, and he used a blade razor and a comb to cut – some would say pull – our hair.

into the camera. Each piece had to be about half an inch longer on each end than the conventional 2¼ inch by 3¼ inch ratio, because it had to be stuck into the camera behind the frame, using small spots of latex to hold it in position. When I had worked out the dimensions, I went back under the stairs and cut up the sheets of X-ray negative film into single pieces. I got hold of a very thin piece of brass as a straight edge, and a Gem razor blade from my shaving set, which was only sharpened on one edge and very handy for jobs

Electric chain saw, Selarang Barracks
This chain saw was originally powered by a petrol engine and I helped to modify it by installing this electric motor. It is being used here to cut seats from palm logs for the Changi theatre.

like that. I did eventually cut up the whole box full of negative sheets, which gave me about 400 single negatives for my camera.

I sealed them up in a Town Talk tobacco tin, a flat tin about 4 inches by 3 inches, using bits of gas cape – which was a waterproof material – to wrap around them. Then I sealed the tin with sticking plaster to try to keep the moisture out. And that film stock lasted me right through, until I had to destroy my camera coming back from the Thai–Burma Railway at the end of 1943. I took about 100

View of Selarang Barracks

I climbed the Selarang water tower to get this all-over view of our first prison camp. Before the surrender it housed the Gordon Highlanders.

negatives with me up the railway but not all of them were exposed. I suppose I took about 100 successful photographs during the time I had the camera as a prisoner of war. I think about 60 of those have survived to the present day.

The chemicals were kept in a selection of small glass bottles which I had over the Selarang area in various places. People had some small bottles of medicine with them and I collected a few of these when they were finished. The chemicals had to be broken down with water, and I kept the original batch buried under one of the buildings to keep it cool. I poured water over it from time to time when I could. Then I would mix up batches of developer and fixer with water, and hide the bottles in different places. I found that you could use one batch of developer about half a dozen times, and then you would see the developing negative turn a kind of milky colour, and you knew it was time to throw it out. The fixer could be used for longer periods, but when I look at some of my negatives now, some deterioration has set in, so maybe there was something I did not do correctly.

The most urgent job was to process the 620 films that I had taken first. These unwound into strips of eight exposures, about two feet long. I set myself up in the space under the stairs with my battery and developing light – the globe wrapped in red bunting. I had my developer in an enamel kidney dish and the fixer in a short half-section of bamboo. The technique was to unroll the film from its paper backing and to hold each end of it while you passed it through the developer in the dish with a kind of see-saw motion, so that the whole of the film at some stage was immersed in the solution. You kept doing that till images started to appear. Then you thought to yourself, 'Are they sufficient or aren't they?' or, 'I'll give it a bit more', or 'I'll stop now'. It was a trial and error method. I just kept going until I thought the negative was of sufficient density to produce a photo. Sometimes it wasn't good, sometimes it was okay. As soon as I decided it had had enough developing, I would pass it through the fixing solution in the bamboo trough, in the same way, and then wash it with ordinary water.

Unfortunately I did not have a thermometer while I was at the Great World, although I did manage to get a clinical thermometer later when I got back to Selarang. Time *and* temperature are important in developing film. But I developed a fairly workable routine under the stairs at the Great World. I used to jot down the times of development. It may be that at one and a half minutes the negatives looked good and at two minutes they were over-exposed. At that stage I had to guess the ambient temperature of the solution and estimate time by counting slowly in my head. It was basically hit and miss, although I eventually developed a formula that achieved the best results possible. With the single negatives I used to catch one corner and put it in the kidney basin, and just lift it in and out with the solution running off it, trying to keep a constant flow over the surface.

At that time I regarded the whole thing as a hobby. It gave me an intense interest in doing something apart from the everyday chores. It wasn't until later years that I realised how important the photos were. But I realised right from the beginning how important it was to keep my camera hidden and to take photos secretly.

I didn't carry my camera in my specially designed kidney belt all the time. Sometimes I would wrap it in a piece of waterproof gas cape, and hide it in a pipe in the ground. There were all kinds of odd places to hide it, although I had to be careful that one of our own people would not pull it out of somewhere by mistake. When I was using single negatives, I would load the camera at night. Then I would hide the camera, and wait for something interesting to photograph. Quite often I would use some of my mates to shield the camera. I'd say 'Today I'm going to try and get a photograph of such and such. Come and get around me a bit.' If there happened to be Japs around, I'd put the camera on someone's shoulder and pretend to be talking while I took the photograph. One technique was to kneel down behind two people, and photograph through the gap between them. That night I would process that one little piece of film, and load up again for the next day.

I tried to keep the camera loaded at all times, because you never knew what might turn up. If I was going somewhere on a working party or a wood-gathering party, I would observe to see if there was anything worth photographing. Then the next day I would bring the camera and get a picture. It might only be something that interested me personally, and perhaps of not much interest to anyone else.

The closest I came to being caught was one day on the Changi aerodrome, where we were working as labourers for the Japanese. There was a little Jap guard on duty we used to call Dopey. He must have had some idea I had a camera, because he came up to me and stood at attention and said 'Okay, you photo, you take photo of me.' That gave me a very nasty shock. I looked at him and said 'Photo? Photo? Oh no, no, no photo.' He said, 'You have camera, camera?' I said, 'Oh, no, no, no camera.' Dopey said, 'Oh, oh, very sorry, very sorry,' and walked away.

Well, I can tell you my heart was in my mouth at the time. I don't think I was concerned about my repercussions if I was caught with the camera. My main concern was not to lose the camera, so I could still get photographic material later on.

The best darkroom and processing set-up I had was back at Selarang, after I had been out on various work parties, and shortly

George Aspinall and Harry Russell at Selarang

Harry Russell (right) and I are standing on the steps leading to the Selarang pump-house where I organised my second dark room.

before I left Singapore to go and work on the Thai–Burma Railway on 21 April 1943. There was a pumping station about fifty yards on the south side of the Selarang Barracks – a concrete building that housed four pumps each driven by a 10-horsepower electric motor. Water was pumped up from the underground tanks to the water tower to provide mains pressure for the barracks complex. I had some electrical knowledge, and I used to help the POW engineers who were assigned to look after the pumps. They let me come and go as I pleased, and the Japanese never went near the place. I actually built a darkroom in the pumping station out of bits of building material and some old groundsheets.

By this time I had managed to get a clinical thermometer, and was able to process my films more accurately.

During the time I worked on the Singapore docks, I noticed that the Japs were using photographic paper to scribble notes on. I thought, 'Hello, that's interesting, I'll see where they are getting that from.' Finally I found a store of two or three hundred boxes of photographic paper, and I smuggled out one box suitable for making contact prints from the 2¼-inch by 3¼-inch negatives.

Back in my Selarang pump-house darkroom, I tried some more experiments to see if I could make photographic prints. I knew that you had to use different developer and fixer for prints, but I only had the same X-ray chemicals to work with. Anyway, I tried them and it worked! I don't know how it worked, but it did. I got two pieces of very clear glass, and a piece of wood with a nice smooth surface on it. Then I put the negative on top of a piece of paper in the developer and watched the image come up to a certain density. It was the same technique I used for the negatives, just stopping the development with the fixing solution and washing with water. The paper was glazed, so I didn't worry about trying to glaze the prints. I used to take photographs of some of my mates and give them copies. I got someone to take a picture of me and a friend, Harry Russell, on the steps leading down to the pump-house, and I still have that print. As a matter of fact, the quality of the negatives has held up better than the prints since the war.

LIFE AT MOUNT PLEASANT

AFTER A FEW WEEKS CAMPED AT THE GREAT WORLD AND WORKING ON THE SINGAPORE DOCKS, the Japanese moved a group of us to the Thomson Road or Mount Pleasant area, where we lived in the partially bombed-out houses that had been occupied by senior British civil servants and their families. Looking back, I now realise that was the best period of being a prisoner of war. In those early days, we'd come to the conclusion that the Japs had so many POWs they didn't quite know what to do with us. The main body of Allied troops was quartered on the Changi Peninsula where they virtually looked after themselves. Some groups of men were sent around the island on working parties, doing various jobs. Our group went to Mount Pleasant to help build a shrine to the Japanese war dead, on top of a hill in the Bukit Timah area of Singapore.

The houses we were quartered in were quite substantial two-storey dwellings. All the furniture and moveable objects had been taken out, but we managed to round up some bits and pieces and made ourselves quite comfortable, although part of the house had

Bomb-damaged Singapore Railway Station
I took this shot on an early working party, showing the shell of the once pretentious Singapore Railway Station. The interested group in the foreground are Chinese workers helping us to fill in shell holes.

been bomb damaged. But the mains power was on, and we even had ceiling fans! There were about fifty or sixty people billeted in each house, so you can see they were quite large mansions. My particular house had two storeys, and the top floor had four large rooms about 25 feet square. Those who didn't want to sleep on the floor knocked up a bit of a bed out of sections of timber and a groundsheet, or some old tenting material tied across in the form of a hammock.

Food was our main problem, although we were eating better than we had been at Selarang. We got a bit more rice – our basic diet – and some vegetables. Occasionally we had an issue of meat from the cold storage in Singapore, which was very welcome, even thought it was a bit off. Some dried fish we got wasn't much better, but we learned that beggars couldn't be choosers. The meat and fish were cooked up, and if it tasted a bit off – well, that was too bad. You mixed it in with your rice and ate it, or went hungry.

We were pretty well left to look after ourselves. There were Jap guards wandering up and down the roads, but they didn't pay much attention to us. They very rarely came into the buildings. Occasionally they'd come in to our cookhouse area looking for something to drink or a cup of tea. These Japanese were front-line troops who weren't really interested in looking after prisoners of war. Eventually they were replaced by second-rate Japanese soldiers and a lot of Koreans, who made life very hard for us. But while we were at Mount Pleasant things were very relaxed in comparison with what was to come.

Every morning we would get up about 6 am, and have our breakfast – if you could call it that – about 6.30. It was what we used to call rice porridge, a very thin glutinous and sloppy form of cooked rice. We ate that and had a cup of tea. If you were lucky, there might be a bit of extra tinned food, like condensed milk, sardines or herrings in tomato sauce which one of us had managed to scrounge while on a working party somewhere. We always used to share whatever came in like that.

Then a group of thirty or forty men were lined up outside before being marched off to work. Not everyone went to work, because

Bomb-damaged house, Mount Pleasant
Our secret radio was operated from a water-storage tank in the roof of this house.

some people stayed behind to cook, clean the house out and even do a bit of gardening to try and grow some vegetables. I suppose of the fifty people in our house, forty would go out to work. We would line up in threes and wait for the Jap guards to pick us up. There'd usually be two of them, and they would count us. They called it *tenko*, and it usually took them two or three attempts before they agreed with each other on the correct number. Then we'd march off down the road about two-and-a-half miles to Bukit Timah village and cut across the Singapore golf course to where they were building the shrine for the Japanese dead. The shrine took the form of a wooden column on top of a steep hill, and our first job was to clear all the trees and scrub from the hill and construct form work for concrete steps. We also worked on road building in the area leading to the shrine.

They thought this shrine was going to be a permanent memorial to the Japanese army. Apparently it is often the practice when building a Shinto shrine to choose an area where you can approach it by crossing a bridge over a watercourse or stream. In other words, you isolate yourself from the rest of the world – that's their philosophy as I understand it. We also worked on the bridge, hammering in timber piles over this bit of a creek which was an overflow from the MacRitchie Reservoir, one of the main water supplies for the city of Singapore. The timber had to be cut down beside the reservoir and floated up to where we were building the bridge. Four or five of us would jump into the reservoir, with one arm around the log and the other paddling to propel the log down the waterway. We worked on these various jobs around the shrine for about six months. It was during this period that we spotted Mah Lee, the Japanese photographer we'd known at Batu Pahat, who turned up as a captain in the Imperial Japanese Army and who was obviously a spy!

As I mentioned, the Japanese front-line soldiers who were supposed to be guarding us at that stage weren't really interested in their job. I used to roam around a bit at night to see what I could find in some of the houses in the Mount Pleasant–Thomson Road area. One particular house intrigued me because I could see a lot of Japanese going into it quite often during the day. When I got in there, I found it was a house for storing radios! Apparently they

Secret radio installed in water tank, Mount Pleasant

This is the AWA Radiola set actually in the water tank. You can see the time switch on the left, which was used to turn the set on automatically for the evening BBC Delhi News.

had gone around the Singapore area and confiscated all the radios they could find. Well, this was a real find, and I had a good look at various types of radio that I thought were okay, and I came back to our house with a radio under each arm. I thought, 'Gee, I'll have to put these somewhere in a hurry.'

Fortunately I was able to get up into the ceiling of the house we were living in. It had been bomb damaged, and there was a ladder up onto the roof where someone was trying to repair it to stop the rain coming in. I took these radios one at a time and hid them in the roof. One of them was an AWA three-band set, about 20 inches wide, 15 inches high, and about 8 inches deep. It was known as a table model in those days. It appeared to be practically brand-new. You see, up to this point we hadn't heard any outside news, or any authentic news at all. We had heard Japanese propaganda telling us that they had taken over country after country after country. I knew it was risky to be caught with a radio, but it was essential to find out what was going on in the world. That particular radio became a very important part of our life then, and later.

We had mains 240-volt power operating in the house, so it was no great problem to get the set working. The difficulty was where to put it so it would not be found by the Japs. There was a water tank up in the roof which had been partly bomb damaged, and the water supply had been cut off. It was an iron type of tank about four feet square, with a little round cover on top. I pulled the cover off and found there was just enough space for me to climb in. I set up the radio inside and got it working, but it was a terrible business climbing into this tank every time we wanted to hear the BBC Delhi News, which came on from 10–10.45 pm. I had some electrical knowledge, and I scrounged around and found a time switch. I installed this so it switched on the set automatically at 10 pm and off at 11 pm. A pair of fine wires led down from the radio to a balcony downstairs, and was connected to an earpiece from a telephone. So every night at 10, one of our intelligence sergeants, Curly Heckendorf, would come over and listen to the news through the earphone, and jot down the highlights. I would sit with Curly and have a listen occasionally just to make sure it was coming through okay. If the radio reception faded or wandered a bit, I would have to go up and climb into the tank to retune the set. It was important to have the set operating in such a way that we didn't have to go near it, because the fewer people who knew about it the better. Once Curly Heckendorf, or whoever was listening, had memorised the highlights, the bit of paper would be torn up and destroyed. Then the news would be carefully circulated verbally.

One story we picked up at that time told how the Japanese midget submarines had got into Sydney Harbour. Some weeks later the Japanese decided to give us a tin of pineapple each, because after the submarines had been caught and blown up, the bodies of the crew were sent back to Japan by the Australian Government. Sometimes the news would get rather exaggerated as it passed from man to man. I remember one chap saying, 'Did you hear about that Jap midget submarine that got right up the Murrumbidgee and shot up Curly Heckendorf's cows?'

The Japanese would try and tell us Sydney had been destroyed by bombing. They would say, 'Darwin, boom boom boom, finish.' We'd say, 'What about Brisbane?' 'Brisbane, boom boom, finish.' 'What about Woop Woop and Bullamakanka?' 'All finish, boom boom boom!' Everything was always to their advantage. They'd captured it already.

I even managed to get some spare parts for the radio. They were valve sets in those days of course, and I had trouble with a couple of the valves. We were working on the Japanese shrine at Bukit Timah at that time and it was not far away from the Singapore broadcasting station. I managed to get over there one night, and contacted a Chinese technician who worked there. I asked him did he have any spare valves for AWA sets? I gave him the serial numbers and he was able to get me a complete new set of valves, which enabled us to keep it going almost to the end of the war.

In fact that particular radio was later smuggled into Changi Gaol. It was actually bricked up in a wall cavity in one of the cells. The walls between the cells were about eighteen inches wide, so we knocked a hole in the brickwork and put the set inside, and connected to the power supply diverted from the cell lighting. A time switch was installed so that the set only switched on at the times of day when the BBC news broadcasts took place. Then the whole thing was cemented in and made to look as though nothing was there. A four-inch nail was driven through the wall and its tip just touched the diaphragm of a headphone within the wall cavity. We listened to it with a kind of stethoscope. All you had to do was put the end of a bit of rubber tubing over the head of this nail, and hold it tight with your finger, and you could hear the transmission. That set did develop a few problems towards the end, and we couldn't hear it. But by that time the war was almost over and we were pretty close to being released. I think the valves must have overheated – but anyway it was not possible to get in and make repairs, so it eventually gave up the ghost.

Talking of ghosts, I read in the papers a few years ago that gaol warders would not go near a certain cell in Changi because they reckoned there were ghosts in it! Changi Gaol is still used as a prison, and it made me wonder whether the old set could still be operating, but I doubt it. The set is probably still in the wall though.

Once I got the radio operating in the roof of the house at Mount Pleasant, the commanding officer of our particular house,

Newspaper report

This newspaper report may or may not be true but certainly our radio could still be walled in.

IT'S reported from Singapore that guides who show visitors around Changi, where so many Australians were imprisoned by the Japanese during the war, won't go into a certain cell. They say ghostly voices can be heard from within.

Local ex-POWs are interested in the report. They think it might be one of the cells in which they secreted a radio tuned to the BBC's Far East broadcasts. They bricked the radio in and connected it to the prison's electricity system.

Volume was so low it could be heard only through a POW doctor's stethoscope. If the set is still operating after all these years, they think the volume might have increased so it can now be heard without a stethoscope!

Captain Bob Howells, said to me, 'Aspinall, you'd better stay in camp instead of going out on work parties. Just keep your eye out for Japs that might come searching round the place.' That suited me fine. I stayed back and involved myself in house duties and doing a bit of gardening. That went on for some months.

The commanding officer of our 2/30th Battalion, Black Jack Galleghan, lived in a house further down the road with a number of his officers. There was also a Japanese guard unit at the house. Then the Japanese decided to evacuate all the senior officers from Singapore and take them away to another country – we didn't know where. I think all senior officers from full colonels upwards were to go. That meant that Lieutenant Colonel Galleghan became the senior Australian officer of the POWs on Singapore Island, and the Japs decided he had to leave the Mount Pleasant area and go back to Selarang Barracks to take charge of the AIF administration of the prisoners of war. After he had been gone a week, Captain Bob Howells said to me, 'I've received word from the Old Man that he wants you to take one of the radios you have to Selarang, because he hasn't got a radio there.'

I left the set in the water tank and took the other one, which had been installed in the roof of another house by that time. It was a similar type of table, or mantel, model set, and it was taken out of its wooden case and broken up into component parts. We thought the best way to get the radio into Selarang was in one of the vegetable trucks that used to go backwards and forwards from Mount Pleasant to Selarang Barracks. The vegetables were in bags or big wicker baskets. The bits of radio were wrapped in hessian bags and distributed in various baskets on the truck. The ploy was that I was supposed to be ill, so I had to sit in the back of the truck to get to Selarang. There was a Jap driver and a Jap guard, and two other Australians, who used to load and unload the vegetables. We drove into Selarang, up to the guard house area, and they just counted us and waved us through. I wasn't feeling too happy about the situation because I knew that if we were searched the radio would have been easily found. I didn't know how long

I was going to be in Selarang, so I had brought all my personal gear in a kitbag, and I had my camera hidden in the canvas belt wrapped around my waist. So it was a risky situation, but we got through okay and I went to where the vegetables were unloaded and hung around until the baskets with the radio components in were hauled off the truck. I said to the chap at the vegetable store, 'There's some gear in these baskets that I've got to get to the Old Man.' The other chaps that were with me helped carry them down to Colonel Galleghan's headquarters. He bid me good day and said, 'Have you brought the radio with you?'

'Yes, Sir.'

'Well, where is it?'

'Oh, we've got it in the bags here. It's partly dismantled and it's got to be put back together.'

Black Jack said, 'Well, get the bloody thing out of here, I don't want to know about it. Take it away and put it back together, and I'll tell you who to give it to.'

Finally we put the set back together, and it was given to a chap called Lieutenant Wright, who was a signals officer and who was given the job of looking after the radio. I helped him get it working and it was christened The Changi Canary. It operated for many years, but I never saw it again. Anyway, that afternoon there was a hell of a commotion with Jap guards running around all over the place, and I thought, 'Oh, they've probably discovered the radio.' But it wasn't that at all, it was the beginning of what came to be known as the Selarang Barracks Square incident, and because I had brought the radio in that day from Mount Pleasant, I finished up being well and truly involved.

THE SELARANG BARRACKS SQUARE INCIDENT

AT 8 AM THE NEXT MORNING, ALL THE PRISONERS OF WAR IN THE SELARANG AREA WERE CALLED out of the buildings and they had to parade in the barracks square, which was an area about two acres and bordered on three sides by seven two-storey buildings, which were our living quarters at that stage. Black Jack Galleghan addressed the parade and said that the Japanese required us to sign a declaration that we would not try to escape under any circumstances. He said that the Japanese were making a number of threats if we did not sign the document. However, he believed that we were being asked to sign against his better judgement and it would not be in our interests to sign.

Well, the Japanese didn't take kindly to that, and they were determined that we would have to sign this no-escape document. So they decided to assemble all the prisoners of war held on the Changi Peninsula in this Selarang Barracks Square area. Most of the British troops were at Roberts Barracks, not far away, and they had to come in with what equipment they could carry. Roberts Barracks was also the main POW hospital, and all the sick had to be moved to Selarang with whatever medical equipment that could be arranged. A lot of the gear was brought on car and truck chassis, pulled and pushed by the troops. It took all day, but by the evening of 1 September, there were 15,400 men assembled in the barracks area that normally housed one battalion – about 1,200 men. I think there were 1,900 Australians in the square and the rest were mostly British.

The seven barracks buildings were really three-storeyed if you counted the roof area, where people camped as well. Different buildings were allocated to the AIF, the British and the Indians – and then there was another building set aside for the very serious hospital patients who had been brought over from the main hospital at Roberts Barracks. This was only three or four months after the surrender. People were just recovering from bullet wounds and amputations or having had their limbs blown off. Some people had been completely or half-blinded, some had chest wounds or were recuperating, with their wounds not properly healed. There were more patients than would fit in one building. Now many of the patients had been pushed or pulled from Roberts Barracks on their hospital beds, which had wheels on them. Some quite enjoyed the ride. The less seriously ill were grouped in the open, and bits of canvas, tarpaulins and old pieces of tent – any coverings that could be found – were put over them. When it was all set up, it looked like a sort of shanty town. The coverings were needed for shade from the intense tropical sun.

The first and most urgent problem we had to face up to was the lack of toilet facilities. Each barracks building had about four to six toilets, which were flushed from small cisterns on the roofs.

But the Japanese cut the water off, and these toilets couldn't be used. The Japanese only allowed one water tap to be used, and people used to line up in the early hours of the morning and that queue would go on all day. You were allowed one water bottle of water per man per day, just one quart for your drinking, washing and everything else. Not that there was much washing done under the circumstances.

We had to dig latrines through the asphalt of the barracks square. There was a piece of equipment we called a bore-hole auger, or digger. It was like a series of shovels welded together with one central bar, and a cross-piece bolted on with U-bolts. Two men used to get on each side of the handles, or with the bigger models, four men could get on each side. They'd just walk around and around in a circle with the bar as the pivot, and the shovels were set up in such a way to form an auger. Now some of these holes were dug twenty and thirty feet into the ground by this method. There was no shortage of manpower and dozens of these holes were dug quite quickly. The area was infested with flies, which carry dysentery and a lot of other diseases, so it was vital that the excreta was covered up so that the flies would not contaminate what little food we had with us. The senior officers had to haggle with the Japanese for some form of covering for the toilets. They allowed in a truckload of timber, which permitted our carpenters to make boxes like you find in country dunnies, to fit over the bore-holes. We called them thunderboxes.

The first day there was no food available, only a few tins of stuff that had been hoarded away for emergencies. But by the end of the second day, I think it was, the Japanese allowed some rice to come in and be cooked. I don't know why – and I don't mean to be hard on English people – but they were appointed as the cooks. There was a small cookhouse at Selarang, and we didn't think much of the way the Pommy cooks treated the rice. Australians had become pretty good rice cooks by then, but the Poms created this gluey mess they called pap. I got about four spoonfuls of it, and I can't say I relished it. But we managed to survive on it. The usual remarks were made . . . you know, 'Who called the cook a bastard? Who called the bastard a cook?' and so on. But we got on well with the British really.

Although it was pretty overcrowded and uncomfortable, we took it as a bit of a joke for the first couple of days. We thought it was something the Japanese would get sick of before we did. The officers had explained to us that we would try to hold out against signing the no-escape document to the fullest extent that we could, but if it looked as though people were going to starve, or there was a serious outbreak of dysentery, we would have to sign the document under duress. Then it would be acceptable. We received information from the junior officers, who moved about among the men explaining different situations that were likely to occur, or were occurring, and who generally kept up our morale and discipline.

On the third morning we had been cooped up in the square, a group of men assembled and were taken away in trucks by the Japanese, together with Colonel Galleghan and some of the senior officers. We heard that they had been taken down to Changi Beach, not far from Selarang Barracks, and made to witness the execution of four prisoners of war who had been caught trying to escape.

The Selarang Barracks Square incident
In the hospital area the wounded were lying under whatever makeshift cover could be set up. There were people with bullet wounds, recovering from amputations and some half-blinded battle casualties.

I heard from people that were there that the men who were shot by firing squad behaved in a very brave manner.

This changed the situation completely. I remember groups of men standing around discussing what had happened, and getting descriptions from some of the people who had witnessed the executions. Everybody was very quiet, and most of the groups were standing facing where the Japanese and Indian Sikh guards were. Up at one end of the square, the open end we used to call it, near a clock tower, there was a group of Indian Sikh rebels who had gone over to the Japanese and were now called the Indian Independent Army or some such name. They were manning machine guns. Now the machine guns only appeared on the day of the executions. I think the Japanese thought that something might happen when we heard about the killings, and they mounted three machine-gun posts. Along the perimeter road that ran around the back of the barracks buildings were quite large concentrations of Japanese soldiers, and some had automatic weapons.

I think the Japs were prepared for some kind of a break-out when we heard of the executions. But our people were sensible enough to know that even if they wanted to make a break, it doesn't take many armed men to keep unarmed men in place. So there was a great air of tension – an air of deep hostility – although it wasn't shown to any great extent.

Eventually Colonel Galleghan asked the officers to bring all the men towards one end of the square. There were several Japanese officers and guards in attendance who could speak English. Colonel Galleghan got up on a flat-topped trailer so he could be seen, and addressed all the prisoners of war. I recall it was something like this: 'As you probably know, there are a lot of men starting to suffer from dysentery, we don't have very much water because the water tower level has dropped to a point where there is very little pressure in the tap, so it's up to you people whether you want to sign the document.'

I think by that stage two men had died the previous night and Colonel Galleghan explained to us that rather than risk further lives – particularly the seriously ill hospital patients – we should consider signing the no-escape document.

The Selarang Barracks Square incident
Fifteen thousand four hundred British and Australian troops were herded into an area which usually held 1200 men. I took eight shots from the AIF building – some from behind the parapet seen in the bottom right-hand corner.

'Please discuss this among yourselves, and I will come back to you in half-an-hour to get your opinion. But my word to you is that we *can* sign this document and save further loss of life, because it would be signed under duress and it would not be binding.'

Well, we stood around in groups and talked about the situation. Most of the discussions I overheard were to the effect that it wasn't much use blokes dying just for the sake of us using our heads a bit.

Then Colonel Galleghan said, 'What conclusion have you come to? Those that wish to sign the document put your hands up, those

7 — BARRACK SQ., SEPT., 1942.

This shot was printed from photographic material on display at the Rabaul war crimes trials and sold in Melbourne by a press photographer as part of a numbered seet of POW photographs. I knew nothing about this until years later. But I have mislaid one of my eight Selarang Barracks Square incident photographs, and I am pleased now to be able to rely on the pirated pictures to complete my own set!

that don't want to sign – just stay as you are.' Colonel Holmes said much the same to the British troops. A majority of hands went up agreeing to sign it. We knew full well that it was just a means of getting out of the situation, and that it was not binding on us in any shape or form.

When we agreed to sign the document, everybody had to line up near the clock tower building, where the Jap and Indian guards were. There were a couple of Japanese sitting at a table with a great stack of forms – pieces of paper about eight inches by six inches, headed 'Imperial Japanese Army', the date, Singapore. 'I,' – then you put your name –'hereby promise that under no circumstances would I attempt to escape.' They may not be the exact words, but they were something like that.

I was one of the ones who voted for signing – not that I had any intention of taking notice of it. I believed I would escape if I possibly could, but it was a pretty hopeless situation because we were surrounded by sea with no boats and nowhere to go.

Well the signing went on from the morning session, right through till late in the afternoon. We all filed past this table and wrote a name on the documents. Some wrote their own names, but there were a lot of Jack Langs and Bob Menzies, and Ned Kelly cropped up quite a few times. Even Judy Garland got a mention more than once, because there was a well-known female impersonator in the Changi Concert Party we called Judy Garland. It was all a bit silly, really. But after you signed the documents you were allowed to go out of the barracks square area, through some Sikh guards, and down to a small valley adjacent to the square where we used to have open-air concerts. We just hung about there for most of the day until everybody had signed, and then everyone was allowed to go back to his own area.

Now I had my camera with me when I was ordered by Black Jack Galleghan to bring the radio into Selarang Barracks from Mount Pleasant. On the second day of the Selarang Barracks Square incident, I was wandering about on top of the AIF building, getting a bit bored and looking for something to occupy my mind. So I thought to myself, I'll take some photos of this situation. I still

We had only one tap working. The queue never stopped. We had to dig latrines by boring holes through the asphalt. The Japs allowed us to build 'thunderboxes' over the holes. A row of them can be seen on the right.

had one of my original rolls of 620 film with me and I decided to use the eight shots to try and capture the remarkable scenes going on in the barracks square. There was a parapet on top of the AIF building which had been damaged by shell fire during the fighting before the fall of Singapore, and it had some bricks knocked out of it. I took my camera out of my kidney belt and, by lying down on the deck of the roof, I could take pictures through the gaps. The Japs were busy watching people from ground level, and I didn't

We had to dig latrines in the square with devices called bore-hole augers. You can see a mound of earth to the right of the hospital area. Our officers were worried that dysentery would break out because of the millions of flies – which eventually happened.

think they could see what was going on up on the roof. There was quite a lot of washing and stuff hanging out, and a lot of men up on the roof. So I started to take photos of the barracks square area from different positions on the top of the building, and from different angles.

The closest area to me was the hospital area, and I took a photo of that. I then gradually swung the camera around and took the eight photos from different positions, overlapping each other to some

This shot was taken from a lower floor of the AIF building, looking over the hospital area. The Japs had Indian Sikh guards manning machine guns at the base of the administration building (top right) in case we tried to break out.

extent. Some were taken from the top of the building, and some were done from the floor underneath to get a better view. I thought I'd done a pretty good day's work then, and I put the camera away and just spent the rest of the day sitting up on the roof watching the different events unfold. And that was how I got the photos of the Selarang Barracks Square incident.

Unfortunately one of the eight shots has been lost, and I think it was one which looked towards the open, clock tower end of the

Some of the worst medical cases were kept in the ground floor of one of the seven barracks buildings – the rest had to make do under tarpaulins and bits of old tents. Without some sort of shade they would have suffered from dehydration in the tropical sun. There was very little water.

square. But as the shots all overlap, it doesn't matter much. As a matter of fact, the Selarang Barracks Square photographs have probably become the best known of my work, and I am sometimes asked what I was thinking when I took them. I never intended them to be an exhibit, or anything like that. It was just the same as if I had been in Australia and I was up the bush somewhere and happened to have a camera with me. I just took a photograph here and there of anything that I thought was of interest. However as

Most of us just stood around discussing the circumstances.

time went on, I began to think that the photographs would help to show to someone who was interested enough some of the conditions that prevailed then.

After we signed the no-escape document and were allowed out of the square, those of us who were left at Selarang were ordered by the Japanese to tidy up. The bore-holes had to be filled in, the thunderboxes dismantled and sent back to a Jap store somewhere. That was quite a big job, because all we had were shovels, a few picks and some tools that were called *chunkels* – a thing like a large hoe. The only thing we had to carry dirt with were wicker baskets with a handle on each side. Other groups were detailed to help take the sick and wounded back over to the Roberts Barracks area, pushing beds on wheels, and carrying gear. It took us about two days to bring the square back to something like it was before the incident occurred.

I managed to get down to the pump-house the night after everybody was sent back to his own area, and processed the film. To my surprise, it came out exceptionally well.

F FORCE

to go by train up to Thailand. Earlier, in 1942, A Force had gone away – we didn't know where – but later we found out they had gone to Burma to begin building the Thai–Burma Railway from that end. We didn't know anything about a railway. The Japanese said that we were going north to rest camps in the hills, where there was plenty of food, and where the sick would be able to convalesce. There would be some work, but it would only be light duties, and we would be much better off than we were in Singapore. Anyway, I went with F Force, but we didn't all leave Selarang Barracks at the same time, and I took a series of photographs of some of our groups leaving. The photos show groups with their baggage waiting for Japanese trucks to come and take them to the Singapore Railway Station. I got a bit cheeky, and took a shot of one of the trucks driving off. There is a Japanese officer in the foreground who appears to be looking at the camera, but I had good cover in one of the barracks buildings. I only managed to get one shot of

175

F Force assembling for the Thai–Burma Railway

The various groups leaving were code-named alphabetically. My group was F Force, shown waiting for transport to take us to our train.

the truck, because this particular Japanese colonel – I think he was a senior interpreter – was walking up and down all the time looking up at us.

I had time to process this film at my pump-house darkroom before my group left by truck for the station. I had my camera hidden in the canvas pocket in my kidney belt. I didn't know how long we were going to be away, and I knew that if you don't process film quickly in the tropics it will never be any good. So I got some little screw-topped medicine bottles and filled them with developer and hypo from the bigger bottles I had buried in the ground after getting them back from the Singapore docks. I was going to try and process any negatives I took as quickly as possible. I had the bottles in my pack with the Town Talk tobacco tin, which had about one hundred pieces of X-ray negative wrapped in waterproof gas-cape material. The only other kit I had was two shirts, two pairs of shorts, a pair of old boots and a slouch hat.

We were searched before we left Selarang, and it was pretty rough. The Japanese made us tip the contents of our kit bags or packs on the ground in front of us, and would come along and kick the stuff about with their boots. If there was anything they didn't like the look of, they might pick it up and have a closer look. But it was pretty casual. They didn't seem to worry too much about what you were actually wearing. Most of our clothes were pretty poor by then and if you were hiding something you wouldn't be silly enough to have it in your pocket where it might be seen. As we got up into Thailand the searches got a bit more severe, but they never really examined our bodies. We tried to study the Jap mentality to some extent and we realised that they did not like to have close contact with us. You sometimes see films where men are searched by being tapped all over the body, or having their shirts or trousers examined. Well, the Japs never did that. They seemed to have a dislike of going too near a white man. I don't think they liked our smell! Of course we weren't always able to wash as often as we would have liked, so they may have had good reason not to stay too close to us. But it did mean they didn't give us thorough body searches.

First truck leaves Selarang with F Force men
The Japanese officer seems to be looking straight at me. I managed to get this shot of our CO Black Jack Galleghan (centre figure in the foreground) farewelling this group of F Force men from Selarang. His adjutant, Stuart Peach, is seen on his right, and Captain Booth has his hand in the air.

I managed to take one photo when we were on our way to the Singapore Railway Station. I was in the second or third truck in the convoy of twelve trucks. I think the Japanese guards knew about some of the shops in the back streets, and we dropped away from the convoy. The driver stopped at a fruit stall, and some of the guards went to buy some. I thought to myself, 'Well, they're not paying much attention to us,' so I took a photo of them. I was standing up in the back of our truck and there was a group standing around me so I managed to get the shot without being observed. But when I look at the photo today I can see some of the Chinese in the foreground who might have known something was going on. One young chap in particular seems to be looking straight at the camera.

When we got to Singapore Railway Station, we were placed into what we called rice trucks – just steel freight cars about twelve feet long and six feet wide. They jammed about thirty-six people into each steel box, with their gear. We didn't worry too much about being packed in so tightly for a start, we were more concerned about being on a train trip going somewhere. But no one could lie down and any sleeping had to be done in a crouched, sitting-up position. The worst part was the heat. Under the full tropical sun, those metal boxes turned into furnaces. Everyone was bathed in sweat. We used to take it in turns sitting near the doorway, which was about five feet wide. We were only allowed to open one door. I don't know what the Japanese thinking was on this, but only the door on the outside of the tracks could be opened – not the one opposite another railway track. It was probably a safety precaution, so that people leaning out would not be hit by a train coming the other way. Anyway, even that one door was a way of getting a breath of fresh air to us.

If people got ill, room was made for them to lie down, but it meant the rest of us were more jammed up. When we got to Gemas on the Malayan Peninsula, we were given a pint of rice and told that was to last us to the next day. We knew Gemas well, because the 2/30th Battalion fought a number of actions there before the fall of Singapore. We passed through the Kuala Lumpur Railway Station on Good Friday morning and were given some watery soup with a suggestion of a bit of yak meat in it. This type of rationing went on through the trip. We didn't get much food at any time.

Street scene on the way to Singapore Railway Station
Our particular driver went through some back streets and the Japanese guards stopped to buy fruit. My friends shielded me while I took this photo. Some of the Chinese in the foreground seemed aware of what was going on!

Toilet arrangements were non-existent. We used to have *benjo* stops. That is the Japanese word for toilet, and it was a case of whenever the train stopped for any reason, you got out and did what you had to do. It was so hot, we generally stayed in the shade of the trucks. But if someone got caught short with a touch of dysentery while we were travelling, we used to have to hold them while they relieved themselves through the open door.

I did take quite a number of photos while we were on the train. The first one was taken in the railway yards at Alor Star in Malaya while we were waiting to allow some military traffic to overtake us. At that stage, most of us were in fairly good physical condition.

At one stopping point in Malaya, some of us managed to get a wash at the steam locomotive watering point – but that was very rare. Mostly we used the stops to relieve ourselves or just sit in the shade of the rice trucks. I tried to take some photos out of the open doorway of the rice-truck, probably more from boredom than anything else. There was a schoolhouse in the distance, and some water buffaloes wandering past, and I took a photograph of the buffaloes.

By the time we got to the Thai border, many of the men had developed dysentery. I think a lot of it was caused by the habit that some developed of not eating all their daily rice ration at once, but putting it to one side and eating a bit at night and the rest in the morning. It tended to go sour, and a lot of people had stomach problems. On one occasion, the train stopped, and a group of dysentery sufferers were relieving themselves in the scrub nearby. Captain Ward Booth, who was a friend of mine and who knew I was taking photos, said, 'Look, get a photo of that, will you?' I wasn't very keen about it because it showed the undignified side of what we had to put up with. But it was taken, and that's that.

As we got further into Thailand, we could see mountains looming ahead, and I took a shot looking along the side of the train with the hills in the distance.

Beside rice trucks at Alor Star Station, Malaya
Our train used to stop for long periods to let military traffic through. It was a relief to get out of those metal rice trucks which were like a furnace. We were still in fairly good condition then. The man looking at the camera is an American, Mal Mawdesley, who worked on one of the Matson line boats, and the chap with his back to the camera is Sergeant Wal Barnes.

I think we were on the train for five days and nights, and then we arrived at a place called Ban Pong. By this stage a lot of people were starting to become weak, mainly through lack of food. We stayed a few hours in Ban Pong, and that was another time I nearly got caught with the camera. There had been one search when we got to the camp, but a couple of hours later they decided to have another one. Apparently they had got wind of some radio equipment

Watering point near the Thailand border
Whenever we could, we used the railway watering points to get a wash. By this time we were close to the Thailand border. A friend of mine, Reg Napper, is looking at the camera.

somewhere, and they were searching desperately for that. A group of Japanese guards burst into our hut unexpectedly. A couple stood at each end of the hut so that nobody could get out, and the four or five inside would grab your gear and tip it on to the ground, and look under your bunk, and anywhere else where stuff might be hidden.

I'd just been to have a *tong* – pouring some water over myself to have a wash – and I'd taken my belt with the camera hidden

Toilet stop in Northern Malaya

Many of us had dysentery through eating contaminated rice. We were allowed benjo (toilet) stops from time to time, otherwise we used to have to hold each other out the open side of the truck while the train was moving!

in it and rolled it up in my clothes. It was just on the bunk in a bundle. The Japs grabbed my pack, emptied it out and kicked my stuff about a bit. Luckily the camera was still inside the belt in its canvas pocket, secured with two little press studs, and it didn't fall out, nor was it noticed. The Japanese had a very single-minded attitude to searching. If they were looking for diaries, they could ignore a revolver – that's going a bit far, but they did seem to have one-track minds when they were searching for something. I was pleased they weren't looking for cameras that day.

Some of our blokes were too sick with dysentery or bouts of malaria to move, so they were left at Ban Pong to join us later. That afternoon we were surprised to be told that we had to march to the next staging camp, carrying what gear we could. We had to leave most of our stuff behind, including a lot of medical supplies, and we never saw it again. Apart from our personal gear, we had to carry the cooking utensils which included metal *kwalis* – big shallow iron pots for cooking rice. We also carried some emergency rations we had brought from Singapore. We only had what we could carry.

The first march was from Ban Pong to Kanchanaburi, a distance of some fifty miles. After a while, we realised we were marching alongside the railway line, and that made us pretty savage. As it turned out, we were beginning a shocking forced march for 190 miles, which was to take us right up into the Three Pagodas Pass area of the railway – close to the highest point of the line, near the Burma border. We covered that distance in eighteen days and it was a terrible time.

Kanchanaburi was the railhead at the time, and that is where the bridge over the River Kwai was eventually built. The track we walked over, I'm told, used to be called the Old Caravan Route from Thailand across into India. We weren't in any state to appreciate the history of the track. The worst part was marching at night. We had to cross lots of streams, some of them quite deep. Parts of the track were stony, and because the monsoon season was starting, there was a lot of deep mud. Then there were the sand flies that would bite you on the forehead and around the neck.

We used to cover about twenty-five or thirty miles each night. We tried to get some sleep during the day, but it was usually impossible

View from train, Thailand
I took this picture looking along the length of the train, by leaning out the open door of the rice truck. Our train journey ended near the base of the mountains just visible in the background.

because the Japanese always wanted to have a *tenko* – a check parade. So every few hours they would line everybody up and count them to see if they were all there. There was nothing much in the way of huts in the staging camps, and we used to try and snatch a few hours' sleep under a bush or anything with a bit of shade.

It was really amazing how, no matter how far away from civilisation we thought we were, Thai traders – mostly women but some men – would come to where we were with baskets of food. It wasn't very appetising, just lumps of glutinous-looking rice and a few

Water buffaloes photographed from train, Thailand

vegetables. We didn't have any money, or even anything much to trade with at that time, so they didn't do much business. I managed to get a couple of photographs of them though.

There were about three hundred in our group, and ten or twelve armed Japanese guards. It would have been possible to give them the slip, but there was nowhere to go. It was jungle all around, and the local population was unfriendly. There was a price on our heads – in fact on a number of occasions some stragglers had fallen behind on the march and had been grabbed by some of the locals and brought

View from train, Thailand

You can see some of the blokes' legs hanging out of the rice trucks on the bottom left of this picture.

up to the Japanese for a reward. They said they'd captured escaping prisoners, which was not the case. If any straggler did fall behind, he got belted by the Japanese guards. I'm sure a number who could not keep up were beaten and left to die in the jungle. Some of the people who dropped back were never seen again and we did hear shots fired on a number of occasions. The guards might have been firing at wild animals, but we suspected a number of our people were shot.

We had about twenty officers with us, and they had to march like everyone else. Most of them were magnificent, particularly the

Dysentery sufferers photographed from train, Thailand
I was asked to take this photograph by Captain Booth, although I wasn't terribly keen. The poor blokes with dysentery had to take any opportunity to relieve themselves when the train stopped.

medical officers. They did everything in their power to encourage and help people who were falling behind. I remember two particularly – Captain John Taylor, one of our doctors, and Padre Paddy Walsh. These two used to watch out for stragglers at the back who were not doing too well late in the night, and help to carry their gear. Some of the officers didn't do this, but they had problems of their own in getting along the track. Fortunately for me, I didn't have any serious problems. I just kept marching and carrying my gear. There were a lot of people worse off than I was. I remember

Thai food vendors following forced march

In the early days of our forced march, Thai women set up little stalls selling rice, vegetables and fruit. I don't think they did much business, as we had no money and nothing much to trade.

Thai food vendors

Although we had little food, there were not many takers for the badly-cooked, glutinous rice these women were offering.

Drying clothes on forced march

We marched by night, and were supposed to rest in the heat of the day. There were no proper staging camps. We spread our gear on bushes to dry. Hec Campbell is about to spread out wet clothes (on the right).

my boots fell to pieces, and I finished the march in bare feet. People tended to help each other. Most of us had been together since we enlisted, and through the various camps we had been in, and I had several good friends who stuck together and we did what we could for each other. And that was how we got by.

Quite often it would rain in the night, and we would try and dry our clothes during the day if the sun was shining. We'd just drape our things over some bushes. I don't really know why, but I did take one photograph of one of these camp sites during the forced march.

Towards the end of the march a lot of us were in pretty bad shape. There was malaria, dysentery and general ill health – mainly due to lack of food. There was no medical assistance for simple things that could have been cured on the spot. We did not have any medical drugs or medicines available at the time – not even an Aspro. Looking back, it just seems like a bad dream, like something that never happened. But it's something that no matter how hard you try, you can't eradicate from your mind.

SHIMO SONKURAI NO 1 CAMP

WE WERE IN A DESPERATE CONDITION WHEN WE ARRIVED AT WHAT WAS TO BE OUR BASE CAMP for the next five months. It was called Shimo Sonkurai, or No 1 Camp. The Japanese had promised us rest camps in the north with light duties and plenty of food. What we found was a filthy, stinking, sodden camp that had been occupied by Indian Tamils. The few huts that were there had no roofs and the so-called latrines were brimming over with water and flowing down the hill towards the camp, and huge shiny green blowflies were buzzing about.

We were given one day to clean up the camp and try to get it into some kind of order before we were ordered out to work. The camp commandant, Lieutenant Fukuda, lined us all up and left us in no doubt as to his intentions and our future. The railway would be built, he said, and every available body would be used to build it. It didn't matter about anybody's life, Japanese or Australian. 'If Australians have to die, if Japanese have to die, the line will be built.' He said if we failed to do the job, they would round up all the native population in the area whether they were Thais, Burmese,

Malays or Indians. The line would be finished no matter how many people had to die in the process.

Our first job was to try and make something of the camp. Most of the *atap* huts were open to the sky and it was already the monsoon season. Our officers asked the Japanese for roofing but were told that there was none available. So we took the sides off some of the huts and made a roof that way. The huts were just made of strips of *atap* palm, woven together. If it was properly done, it could be made waterproof. It took two weeks to get the camp into some kind of order, but not everyone was allowed to work on it. Work began immediately on roads and tracks to allow vehicles to get supplies up in to the area before we could start work on the actual railway line. We had to cut down trees and make a corduroy road out of the trunks in the bad places. But the whole area was bad, it was just one muddy quagmire. We had to build about six miles of road in our immediate area so that vehicles could get through, and it was five or six weeks before we started on the railway embankment.

My group, F Force, was one of the most northerly working parties on the railway in Thailand, near the Burmese border. It was known as the Three Pagodas Pass area, because of three small Buddhist pagodas situated right on the highest point of the line. F Force occupied several camps around there. Shimo Sonkurai No 1 was the biggest base camp, and then there was Naka Sonkurai No 2 Camp and Kami Sonkurai No 3 Camp. Unfortunately the Japanese administration decided that we would be administered from Singapore and the Burma people would get their supplies from the Burma end. No one seemed to know where our food was supposed to come from. Although it was supposed to come from the south, it often did not arrive. It was necessary for some of our men to go north into Burma, and south down the line, to try and get some rice which had to be carried many miles over muddy, slippery tracks. Some Japanese ration trucks were getting through, but they were supplying their own troops in Burma and refused to let us have any of those supplies. Some of our officers helped to carry rice to the camp while the men were out on working parties building roads and the railway embankment.

You can imagine the state of the food sent from Singapore or Bangkok, when it did arrive. Occasionally we would get cases of prawns, sent unrefrigerated of course. They would just be putrified shells, eaten out by maggots. Our medicos said that if this mess was thoroughly boiled it could be eaten and would give us some protein. So that was made into what we called prawn soup. At least it gave the rice a prawny flavour . . . or more likely the boiled-up maggots provided the flavour, because they had been living on the prawns. We ate anything we could get our hands on, it didn't matter how bad it tasted, as long as you could eat it.

Apart from the eternal rice diet, we occasionally got some yak meat. Now a yak is an animal very similar to a bullock, and wooden boxes of this stuff came up from the south. By the time it reached us it was virtually jumping out of the box with maggots. The cooks used to dump the lot into big cauldrons of boiling water, maggots and all. The maggots were skimmed off the top, and after a day of stewing, the meat was fit to eat. Not that there was much of it, just a small piece of meat to mix in with our rice. It was a very coarse-grained meat and we used to shred it up to make it go a bit further and change the taste of the rice. We had been living with rice for so long, and its flavour was so monotonous, that we would do anything possible to change it – even leaves off a tree if they were reasonably edible – just to change the taste.

The Japanese had a peculiar attitude to our rations. We always had a number of men who were too sick to go out to work. So the Japanese would count the number of men not working and subtract that number from the issue of rice or vegetables or any foodstuff made available on that day. Their idea was that if a person was sick, he didn't require food. So if there were fifty men sick on a particular day, we were fifty men's rations down. That's where our internal organisation took over. The cooks would be told how many men had to be fed and some people we called rice quantity experts would look at a dixie or a bucket of rice very closely and say, 'There's enough for three-quarters of a pint, or half a pint per man,' depending on how many had to be fed.

Then everyone would file past and get their measure of rice. If there was some left over, the experts would look at it again and say, 'There's three spoonfuls here for 500 men.' So we'd all file through again for three spoonfuls. Sometimes there wasn't enough for everyone to get more, so a back-up system was organised. Maybe twenty men would get four spoonfuls of rice and it would be done in alphabetical order. The next meal, if there was any left over, it carried on so that those who didn't get extra rice in the morning would get it at the evening meal. We didn't waste a single grain of rice. The Malay word for 'more' is *lagi* and some of us called the back-up system the 'leggy'. Someone would say 'What "leggy" letter are we up to?' 'Oh, I think we're up to L,' and so on. We were very conscious of food – we lived and talked about food. The chance

Washing platform, Kami Sonkurai Camp No 3
We built bamboo platforms in some of the small creeks to help us get clean after a day's work on the railway. We had to be extremely careful not to get any water in or near our mouths because cholera was about at that stage. The chap with the slouch hat standing in the middle of the platform is a friend of mine, Carl Odgers.

of getting three spoonfuls of extra rice was quite a highlight of the day. The method was rigidly applied and people didn't try to jump the queue. If you couldn't be there to get your leggy, one of your mates would make sure you didn't miss out. And the sick got their fair share too, despite the Japanese policy of not providing food for them. Some of our senior officers pointed out to the Japanese that they would get their railway built more quickly and efficiently if they fed us properly and gave us better accommodation and amenities. This never seemed to have much effect on the Japanese, they just wanted that line built quickly no matter how many people died. I formed the impression that they didn't want anyone left alive after it was built.

Not everyone went out to work. A skeleton staff – and that's a sick joke under the circumstances – of cooks stayed behind, helped by sick men on light duties. This meant cleaning up around the camp, trying to repair the *atap* on the huts, or possibly doing a bit of washing for some of their mates. But most of them were too ill to do much, as they were suffering from malaria, beriberi – or recovering from dysentery and, in some cases, cholera. If cholera was about, a great deal of effort had to be put into boiling all water used for cooking, washing and drinking. The light-duty men had to carry water up from the creek, make fires and boil water so that the working parties could fill their water bottles for the next day. There also had to be cauldrons of boiling water near the food distribution point, so that eating utensils could be dipped in boiling water. In addition, all food had to be scrupulously boiled, and covers of banana leaves made to prevent the huge green blowflies contaminating it.

A typical day would begin at around 5 am Tokyo time – because all the Japanese-occupied areas worked on Japanese time whether it got dark at 4 pm, or light at 5 am. We used to sleep on bamboo sleeping platforms that ran along the full length of the huts, a foot or so above the ground. We just lay on the split slats of bamboo, and if you were lucky enough you might have a bit of groundsheet or a shirt to put between you and the slats. Breakfast was a pint of rice and we would wash and scald out our dixies to take more rice for lunch with us – although sometimes our lunch would be brought out to us by some of the light-duties men. Whatever happened it was still rice! Dress was varied. You might have the remains of a pair of shorts, but most of us wore a loin cloth or G-string made from a bit of tin or any material we had scrounged. Most of us still had our slouch hats, or some form of headgear, but our boots had pretty well disintegrated by then. Some had made up sandals or thongs, but if you worked in the mud you ended up in bare feet.

We'd be marched off to the work site, which was mainly embank-ment work in the Shimo Sonkurai area. Each man, or small group of men, would be allocated so many cubic metres of earth to be moved from A to B. This might mean digging out the side of a hill and transferring the soil to the embankment of the railway. We mostly worked in gangs of eight to ten men. Some would be digging the earth out with *chunkels*, which were like big garden hoes. The dirt would be placed in little wicker baskets with a handle on each side and carried to the embankment. So there would be one group digging and loading the baskets, another group carrying the baskets, and the rest of the gang spreading out the earth on the railway embankment. The day's quota was marked out on the ground for each gang.

In the early days, the Japs would measure out the area to be moved and filled with their bamboo rods, and if the work gang finished early, they could get back to camp first. But the Japanese woke up to this and just enlarged the area to be filled. So people who worked quickly did themselves a disfavour. We worked out that you didn't rush at the job to try to get back early, you just kept plodding along to finish your job by 5 or 6 o'clock at night. Those who finished early might help another group to complete their day's allotment so we all got back to camp together.

We worked from daylight to dark, so it was usually night by the time we got back to camp. We would go down to the creek and try to wash some of the mud off ourselves, and wash our work clothes and hang them up in the faint hope they might be dry by the morning. Then we'd line up for our pint of rice, perhaps flavoured with some prawn soup or yak meat soup, or anything that happened to be available that day. Sometimes there was a small piece of dried fish, which had a peculiarly pungent smell. We called it 'Modern Girl'. If the cooks had been particularly enterprising, they would get hold of some oil – red palm oil or maybe some ghee. Then they would pat the rice into little cakes and fry them in the oil. They gloried in the name of 'doovers', which meant they could be anything. But at least it changed the taste of the rice slightly. Some of the more innovative cooks would burn grains of raw rice, and stew it up into a concoction we called coffee. It looked like coffee, but it didn't taste much like it unless you used a lot of imagination.

By the time you finished your meal it would be getting late, and if you had any cuts or abrasions, or anything the matter with you, you went down to an area called the sick bay where the medical officers and their orderlies were. They didn't have much to give you, but there might be some antiseptic to put on your wounds. The Japs did supply a fair bit of Mercurochrome, which stains the skin bright red. If you had a bruise or cut, you would wash it out thoroughly and it would be plastered with Mercurochrome. Just about everyone in the camp went around with Mercurochrome on them somewhere.

Then you would go to your bunk area, which was a bamboo platform, built above the dirt floor and just wide enough for a man to lie down, running down the entire length of a 300-yard-long hut. You'd probably have personal space on this platform about a yard wide if you were lucky. You'd try to get some sleep if you could, because it was up at 5 am and out to work again.

I think we survived because we were determined that we were going to get home and that we could put up with anything the Japs threw at us, no matter how hard or tough it was, in order to get home. Everyone helped each other as much as he could, and that was one of the things that got most of us through. There were one or two cases of men behaving selfishly, like trying to get a bit more food than the others, but these incidents were rare. If something like that did happen, the individual concerned would be singled out and given a quiet talking-to by one of us – not necessarily an officer or NCO. He'd be told to pull himself into line or he'd get a belting from his own people. But that wasn't necessary very often. Most did the right thing, and that's how we kept together and survived.

It was Japanese policy to segregate the officers from the men, and they lived apart from us. In the early stages of the work, some of the officers came out to the work parties and tried to argue with the Japanese that certain individuals weren't fit enough to work, and generally tried to look after the interests of the men on the job. I think the Japanese got sick of this and ordered the officers to remain in camp. Some of them took their badges of rank off and went out on work parties to take the place of sick men. But others just stayed in camp all the time. One senior officer in particular was famous for sitting under his mosquito net in camp and doing nothing. He lay back there issuing orders and making life difficult for his own officers, and for the rest of us. He's dead now, but I won't name him. However there's one particular incident that I can't forget.

There wasn't much opportunity to scrounge extra food up in the Three Pagodas Pass area, because there were few local settlements. However, one night we went out to a Thai hamlet and rounded up one of their yaks and brought it back. We slaughtered it in the jungle, just above the camp, and buried the skin. The rest was cut up into small pieces and smuggled in to the cookhouse and boiled up overnight. The hospital patients were given a good feed of soup, with meat in it. The remainder was mixed with rice. It all had to be done very quickly, and we were in cahoots with the cooks. Unfortunately, this senior officer I mentioned earlier found out about it and he threatened that if the people responsible for killing the yak did not come forward, he would personally find out who they were and hand them over to the Japanese! He was scared that there would be reprisals if the Japanese found out we had stolen a yak from the local people.

The officers formed a canteen fund, which was used to supplement rations for the sick. It is a known fact that very few officers died on the railway, compared with the one-in-three death rate of the men. But most behaved well – even taking bashings from the Japanese for insisting that conditions be improved. All the doctors were magnificent. You won't find any ex-prisoner of war who has anything but the highest praise for the way the medicos looked after us. But there were some senior officers who made no effort whatsoever to try and improve our conditions on the railway.

One of the things that made conditions difficult was the attitude of the Japanese and Korean guards. There was a great deal of face slapping and beating with bamboo sticks for apparently no reason. You could never tell when you were going to cop it. I suppose it was a reflection of their own military system, which was very brutal by our standards. There was a lot of corporal punishment. A senior officer would slap or belt a junior officer. That officer would bash a sergeant, who would bash a three-star private, who would in turn belt a two-star private, and on down to the lowliest private. He would take it out on a Korean guard, who would then bash the prisoners of war! We were the last cab off the rank in status, although the poor Asians used as forced labour were even worse off than we were. They died in tens of thousands on the railway. At least we had our military discipline. They had nothing.

One incident at Shim Sonkurai was most odd. Like everyone else, I'd had my fair share of bashings when work quotas had not been filled. But one day – for a reason I have forgotten – the Korean guards made us stand in two lines facing each other, and we were ordered to bash each other! Well, we started off trying to make a show of it, but not doing each other much harm. Then the chap opposite me gave me a couple of hefty thumps. I gave him a couple of good ones back and we said to each other, 'Hey, ease off a bit!' We did a lot of arm swinging and shouting, but not much actual contact was made. If one of the Koreans thought that you were not bashing your mate hard enough, he would come along and take over with his stick. So you had to make it look as realistic as you could.

While this was going on, some Japanese railway engineers came along, and didn't like what they saw. They made the Koreans stand opposite each other, and put them in the same situation. We just stood there while *they* were made to bash each other, with the engineers getting stuck into them if they thought the Koreans weren't hitting each other hard enough.

That was a talking point for quite a few days afterwards.

CHOLERA HILL

ONE OF MY MOST TRAUMATIC PHOTOS IS THE ONE I TOOK OF CHOLERA HILL, AT SHIMO SONKURAI Camp No 1, on the Thai–Burma Railway. Every time I look at it, many memories come flooding back. It was by far the worst time on the railway for our group in F Force, and it is really unbelievable that any of us lived through it. We knew there was cholera about, and when it hit our camp those who contracted the disease had to be put in isolation in a special area. It became known as Cholera Hill, and there is a whole story in this one photo.

The two tent flies on the left are the cholera hospital. The tents were erected over a split bamboo floor and whatever could be done for the cholera patients – which wasn't much – was done there. Cholera is an awful business. A man can be dead within hours, as the body just hurls out all its fluid in violent explosions of vomiting and diarrhoea. A cholera patient can lose half his body weight in hours, and become totally unrecognisable, even to his friends. The deterioration could be that quick. One of our cooks, a heavily built man we used to call Two-Ton Tony, got cholera, and when his friends came up to the hospital tent to see him only some hours after he had come in, he had lost so much weight they didn't recognise him. He realised what had happened, and I think the shock of that helped to kill him.

The doctors used to tie bamboo identification disks on to the patient's wrist so they would know who it was. The doctors managed to organise some saline intravenous drips, by using stethoscope tubing and hollow bamboo needles, and saved quite a few that way. But many died.

Outside the 'hospital' was a bamboo stretcher, used to carry bodies over to the holding tent – which can be seen in the middle of the photo – until they could be taken away to be burnt. That used to take place on the far right of the picture, where there was a big pit. A layer of bamboo would be cut, and the bodies carefully placed on the bamboo, and then more bamboo laid on top. This would be set alight to cremate the bodies.

In the immediate foreground is the operating table used for amputations, tropical ulcer treatment and any other emergency operations that had to be done. There is a box on the table which contained the few instruments that the doctors had, which were sterilised by boiling them up in a bucket over a fire. There is also a piece of bamboo attached to the fork of the tree over which a mosquito net used to be stretched to try and keep the blowflies away during an operation.

An access road can be seen at the rear of the photo. A heap of logs is just visible behind the road. They were telegraph poles for the line, about twenty-five to thirty feet long, with the thick end about a foot in diameter. It took eight or ten men to carry one log. We

General view of Cholera Hill, Shimo Sonkurai No1 Camp

This photograph brings back many traumatic memories. It shows the cholera isolation hospital area at Shimo Sonkurai No 1 Camp. Cholera patients were housed under canvas on the left of the photo. In the centre is the operating table used for amputations, ulcer treatment and post-mortems. A mosquito net was hung over the cross bar above the table to try to keep the blowflies away. The box on the table contains what surgical instruments were available. If someone died, the body was carried on a bamboo stretcher (there is one to the right of the hospital tent) over to the small holding tent on the right. Later the bodies were burned in an area towards the back right-hand side of the picture. There is an access road running across the back of the picture, and a pile of logs can be seen. These were telegraph poles for the railway. I think it is quite remarkable that there is so much detail, as I was using coarse-grained X-ray material at this stage, and my developing chemicals were becoming weak through too much use.

did have elephants working in our area, but if they couldn't shift a particular log, the Japanese would call on the POWs to come and shift it instead.

So this particular photograph brings back lots of memories to me, and I find it difficult to talk about, even more than forty years on. Many of my mates made that final journey from the cholera tent hospital over to the holding tent, and then to the cremation pit.

I didn't get cholera, but I did get dengue fever and malaria. One night, while I was having a bout of malaria, I felt my heart stop! I was having a kind of malarial seizure, with a high temperature, perspiration and so on, and my heart just seemed to stop beating. It is a difficult sensation to describe, and it only lasted for a few seconds. You can usually feel your pulse within yourself – like the sound of your heart beating inside your head. When that stops, you notice it. I became very rigid, and I was half delirious. I suddenly jolted myself awake, and started to think about what had happened. I did speak to our medical officer about it and he said it was a symptom of cardiac beriberi. I think that was the worst moment I had as a POW. I was also on the verge of cerebral malaria, but I recovered from that.

I was lucky not to be troubled with tropical ulcers. I did develop a couple of small ones on my leg towards the end, but fortunately they did not 'take off' and they were eventually treated and healed when I got back to Changi. But next to cholera, ulcers were the worst thing that could happen to you. They would start as a small scratch, or sore, and just eat into your flesh and keep on growing and growing. One of the methods used to treat them was to scoop out the bad flesh of the ulcer with a spoon sharpened on one side.

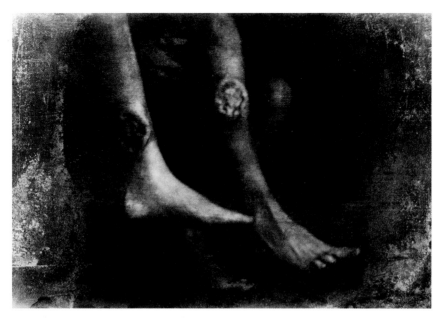

Tropical ulcers in early stage of development

One of our surgeons, Major Bruce Hunt, asked me to take some photos of tropical ulcers forming on the legs of some of our blokes.

Tropical ulcers might stay this size for some weeks, and then they would 'take off' and spread from knee to ankle. Then the ulcer patients would have to have their legs amputated, sometimes without anaesthetic. A few survived, but many died from the shock of the operation.

It was desperation treatment really. The idea was to get back to the good flesh, in the hope that it would heal. I used to sharpen spoons for one of our surgeons, Major Bruce Hunt. I had a little honing stone, and would get hold of a solid tin spoon and sharpen the edge on one side, right around to the handle. This sharp edge was used as a scalpel. Major Hunt became quite adept at using this spoon. He would cut by moving the spoon backwards and forwards, at the same time scooping out the bad flesh from the ulcer. It was an excruciatingly painful procedure, of course, and there were virtually no anaesthetics. I sometimes used to help to hold blokes down on the operating table while their ulcers were scraped, so I couldn't help but see what was happening.

By this time I was determined to try and get some photographs of some of the terrible things that were happening to us, to be used as evidence against the Japanese if we ever got home. I took several photos of some of my friends' legs affected by ulcers. Unfortunately they did not come up too well, but you can see the extent of the ulcers on the legs. Often an ulcer would just stay the same size for weeks on end, and then it would suddenly take off and spread right down a man's leg from knee to ankle in a few days. If it got too bad, the leg had to be amputated. On several occasions, I helped our chief surgeon Major Hunt, Dr Stephens and Dr Cahill by holding a patient down while amputations were done without an anaesthetic.

I only know of one man who survived an amputation under these conditions. As far as I know he's alive today, but most died from the shock of the operation. Even so, many of the ulcer sufferers would be begging the doctors to amputate their legs. Some of the bad cases had the shinbone exposed. You could see their tendons clearly. Sometimes the bone would go black and start to break down and rot. Then the flies would get in and lay their eggs, and the maggots would actually be in there, feeding on the bone marrow. They would start to work up, all the way up the leg. It used to drive blokes off their heads with pain. In my estimation that was the worst thing that could happen to you. Imagine these things gnawing at the marrow of you – bloody maggots gnawing at the marrow in your bones. They would beg the medical officer, 'For Christ's sake cut me leg off – I can't stand this anymore.' That was why a lot had to have their legs amputated.

No matter what was happening to our health, be it ulcers, cholera, beriberi, malaria or dysentery, the work on the railway went on. The Japs used to raid our hospitals for the sick, and declare them fit for work. One of my best known photographs is called 'Three Fit Workers', taken outside our so-called hospital. The man on the right can't do his shorts up because his stomach is so swollen with beriberi, and the middle chap's legs are virtually the same diameter from his ankles to his thighs with water beriberi. The man on the left has the same complaints, malnutrition and beriberi. Yet these men were declared fit to work by the Japanese.

I took another photo of a larger group of 'fit' workers outside the hospital, but it has not come out so well. I had some problems with the emulsion of the negatives sticking together in the damp, tropical heat and the group shot has been badly affected. But you can see enough to recognise some individuals and get an idea of how sick they were. Most of these men did not survive the railway.

There are two photos from this period which have not survived and I much regret that they have been lost. A number of Australians tried to escape from the railway, and were caught and brought back to camp. The Japs made them dig a hole about six feet deep and eight feet square, and the men were put in it and bamboo trunks were criss-crossed over the top so they couldn't get out. There may have been five men in the pit, it is difficult to recall exactly. They were often left alone for hours on end, and I managed to get fairly close without attracting the attention of the Japanese. I took a photo, and you could see two men sitting in the bottom of the hole, looking up at me. I remember one of them said, 'Get the hell out of there or you'll be down in here too.' The other photo showed the pit from a wider angle. These pictures were sent to Rabaul for the Japanese war crimes trials after the war but I have never seen them since.

I didn't carry the camera with me all the time on the railway. I had various hiding places for it in the different camps we were in. Our huts had bamboo sleeping platforms, about eighteen inches off the dirt floor. I would sometimes add an extra piece of bamboo framing under my particular bed area, and hide the camera there. I would use a bamboo section that had a cavity big enough to take the camera, and split it into two halves. Then I would tie it back in place with the camera inside. The main reason why I used my own bed area was that if the camera was ever found, somebody else wouldn't be blamed. That is also why I didn't involve anybody else in my photographing activities. For that reason, I got the name of being a bit of a loner. But it wasn't only the camera. I was also mixed up with secret radios from time to time, and I didn't want to involve anyone in case I got caught.

The Japanese military police, the *Kempeitai*, had well-known methods if they wanted information. They would grab anyone associated with a suspect, and say, 'What do you know about this, or that?' If they didn't answer them, torture was applied, and I wouldn't expect anyone to put up with torture on my behalf because I had been doing something the Japanese didn't like. So for that reason, I kept to myself quite a lot.

I tried to operate the camera on the railway in the same way I had in and around Selarang Barracks, on the Changi Peninsula in Singapore. I would load the camera with one strip of X-ray film at night, so it would be ready if I needed it. But things were more difficult up on the railway. I couldn't just take a photo whenever I felt like it. I had to wait until there were no guards about, and sometimes the jobs I did made it impossible to carry the camera. Then I had medical problems such as dysentery and beriberi. Sometimes I wouldn't take a photo for weeks on end. And sometimes I would take a picture – usually if we went to a new location – and it wouldn't be possible to process it for a week or so.

At Shimo Sonkurai No 1 Camp, I would try and get down to the creek at night, unload the exposed piece of X-ray negative and reload the camera. As well as medicine bottles of developer and fixer, I had one little bottle of latex or raw rubber, and I daubed a little bit on each corner of the unexposed film and glued it in place in the back of the camera. I used to get well away from the light of the campfires – we had no electric lights of course. It was best if there was no moon, but I was a bit worried about starlight as well. I used to sit with an old groundsheet over my head, and get my bottles of chemicals and pour them into small sections of bamboo, and begin to process the latest photo. As I immersed the negative in the developer, I would tap my foot and count, 'One . . . two . . .

Three 'fit' workers at Shimo Sonkurai No 1 Camp

The Japanese considered these men fit for work. The man on the right can't do his shorts up because his stomach is swollen with beriberi. Ossie Jackson (centre) has wet beriberi in his legs, which are virtually the same diameter from his ankle up to his thighs. Benjamin Pearce (left) is also suffering malnutrition and beriberi.

More 'fit' men at Shimo Sonkurai No 1 Camp

This negative was badly damaged, but it is still possible to see the desperately emaciated condition of men the Japanese considered fit workers for their railway construction.

three . . . four . . .' and try and judge the timing as well as I could. It generally took about two-and-a-half minutes, or a few seconds either way. If the negative had a hazy, milky look about it, it meant the image was under-developed. If you over-developed, you got a very clear negative, with virtually no contrasts on it at all. I was able to judge the best times to get good dark images by trial and error. After fixing the film in the other bamboo container, I would just hold on to a corner of it and wash it in the stream. Then I'd wipe it over with a bit of a handkerchief I had – like a sponge – and hang it on the shoot of a bamboo bush or tree with a pin or a bit of wire.

I couldn't afford to wait until it was completely dry, but I did have a few bits of blotting paper that got used over and over again. I would put the latest negative between the two pieces of blotting paper and put it away in the Town Talk tobacco tin that had the unexposed strips of film, as well as the ones I had already processed. Then the next night, or maybe a couple of nights later, I would open the tin again, and remove the negative from between the two sheets of blotting paper and give it a bit of a wipe over if there was a moisture mark on it. Then I would add it to the store of finished negatives, wrapped in a piece of gas cape, which was an oilskin type of material. And that's what I did every time I took a photo.

Unfortunately the last group of photos I took up on the railway didn't come out so well. I think the developer was getting exhausted, and the wet season didn't help either. Often my gear was wet for weeks on end, and some of the negatives got stuck together with the humidity. Later, when the films were recovered and brought back to Australia, it was impossible to separate them, and some were completely ruined.

I managed to keep my camera with me for the whole time I worked on the Thai–Burma Railway, and I had hoped to get it back to Singapore. But that was not to be.

By November 1943, we had finished building the railway embankment. Then a group of Australians from A Force on the Burma side came through laying rails. They worked day and night. All of a sudden a motor vehicle with railway wheels on it appeared, pulling a few trucks. That was the first traffic we saw on the railway. Finally steam locomotives were running, pulling trains in both directions. When it got to this stage we thought, 'Oh well, surely we'll be getting away soon.' Then out of the blue one day we were told to pack all our belongings, all our cooking gear and everything else, and start marching back down the line to a place called Nikki about eight miles from where we were at Kami Sonkurai No 3 Camp. There we boarded a train which had been transporting horses, presumably packhorses, for the Japanese army in Burma. That was how we set off back down the railway that had caused the deaths of so many thousands of Asian labourers and Allied prisoners of war.

At least we rode back by train, a considerable improvement on the terrible forced march on the way up. Not that it was a ride without worries. We knew that many of the bridges had been badly built on purpose by the Australian and British work gangs, who had carefully put nests of termites into the wooden piles, and other little tricks to sabotage the construction. We had a few anxious moments with the train creaking and groaning over some of the trestle bridges. We had come up from Singapore in rice trucks, and we came down from Nikki in cattle trucks. When we got to Kanchanaburi – we called it Kanburi – I took my last photograph as a prisoner of war, but I didn't know it was to be the last at the time.

Kanchanaburi was the beginning of the Thai–Burma Railway. But when our train got there, the Japanese didn't expect us apparently. We didn't know whether we would be continuing on the train down to Singapore, or whether we would go into camp at Kanchanaburi. We hung about, sitting beside our train, for half a day or so. There weren't many Jap guards about, so I took a photo of our train of cattle trucks, beside another train of rice trucks. The men are just lying in the shade of the train waiting for something to happen. You could always tell if a bunch of Australians were on the move by the billy cans hanging out the doors and windows of the train. They were used as rice buckets and had been manufactured in Selarang Barracks out of steel lockers. Anyway, after what seemed a long time, the Japanese decided to move us into camp at Kanchanaburi while they made up another train to take us to Singapore.

I had time to process this last photo at Kanchanaburi, although my chemicals were getting very weak. I had run out of film by that stage, because the monsoon weather had made the unexposed sheets stick together in a gluey mess and I couldn't separate them. I decided it was time to dump the chemicals, after I processed the last bit of film I could use. I knew I had plenty more X-ray negative material and developing chemicals back at Selarang.

When we got off the train, all our gear was searched, and the sick were taken away to hospital areas. I had my camera with me hidden in my kidney belt, which was lucky for me as it turned out. Anyway, I helped carry one of our chaps on a stretcher. He had had his leg amputated and the stump was all puffed up and swollen, and

The last photograph: two troop trains, Kanchanaburi, Thailand
You could always pick Australians on the move by the billy cans about the place. We were on our way back to Singapore and we stopped at Kanchanaburi. Unfortunately the searches by the Japanese military police, the *Kempeitai*, became so tough that I had to destroy my camera shortly after this photo was taken.

he was in a bad way. Four of us carried him on a piece of hessian stretched over two bamboo poles, and we went straight down to the so-called hospital area with him. It turned out that the searches at Kanchanaburi were being done by the Japanese military police, the *Kempeitai*, and they were much more thorough than we had been used to up on the railway. As it happened, I missed the body search because I had been helping carry the chap with the amputated leg. One of my friends came to me later and said, 'Have you still got that

218

bloody camera?' I said, 'Yeah.' He said, 'Well look, if you'd been in that search we just had, they'd have got you for sure.' So I thought to myself, 'Gee, things are getting tough.' I was a bit depressed by losing some of the film through the moisture caused by the monsoon, and I didn't think I could get my hands on any more negative material in the immediate future. Also I didn't want to push my luck too far.

I decided to break my camera up. I pulled it to pieces as much as I could, broke it up, mutilated it, and threw it down a deep well – and that was the end of the camera. I got the Town Talk tobacco tin with all my exposed film in it, and hid it in the canvas pocket in my kidney belt that the camera had been in. I had to be on the lookout, because the *Kempeitai* would suddenly line a lot of people up and search them. When this happened, or looked as though it might happen, I took the tin out of my belt and put it down on the ground somewhere, or shoved it under some grass and leaves. Fortunately, just as we were about to get on the train to go back to Singapore, that particular *Kempeitai* unit suddenly disappeared to go off annoying other people somewhere else. From then on we had various searches from time to time, but nothing like the *Kempeitai*.

I felt very sorry later on that I'd broken the camera up. I thought we were going to have a really thorough search when we got on the train to Singapore. But the *Kempeitai* people had gone, and I could have taken half a dozen cameras on the train. Later on, I could have taken more photos. But it seemed the right thing to do at the time, and that's all there is to it. Only a few of my friends had been aware that I had a camera and had been taking photos on the railway. I don't think they paid much attention to it. I just think they thought, 'Oh, it's just something he's doing, it will probably come to nothing . . . he's just amusing himself.' I think a lot of them had that attitude. And that suited me!

Less than half the group in F Force that I was with got back to Singapore. Six or eight trains took us up to Thailand and they only needed two or three trains to bring us back. I well remember the night we got back to Selarang, which was like coming home to us. Our commanding officer Black Jack Galleghan was there to meet us. We must have looked a straggly mob in comparison to the group he'd farewelled. He was visibly upset. Up till that time they had had no word, no idea, of what had happened to us.

Now those who had stayed in Changi were mainly people who had been wounded during the action – or who had had amputations or something very radically wrong with them. The Japanese had gone through everyone who looked fit enough to work and taken them away. So the ones who stayed in Changi looked pretty bad to us when we left. When we came back, they looked pretty good! Not that they were in good physical shape either, but they were a lot fitter than we were. They were very good to us too. They gave us everything they possibly could, any little thing they had – maybe an extra shirt or spare pair of shorts, or a little tin of food they were keeping for an emergency. All these things came out and were given to the people that came back from the railway.

I had an ulcer on my leg and was transferred to the hospital building in Selarang for treatment. The bad part of the ulcer was cut out, and I was pleased, because it was starting to get bigger and if I hadn't got off the railway when I did, I probably would have lost my leg.

SABOTAGE AND SURVIVAL

IN MAY 1944, NOT LONG AFTER THE ULCER ON MY LEG HAD HEALED, THE JAPANESE ORDERED US to move from the Selarang Barracks over to Changi Gaol. A lot of people who hear the name Changi think that we were in Changi Gaol all the time, but we only spent the last year of our captivity there. Changi Gaol had been occupied by civilian internees, and they were cleared out and sent to a camp in River Valley Road. There wasn't room for everyone actually inside the walls of the gaol, and a lot of the *atap* huts we had been living in around Selarang were dismantled, cut up into sections and moved some three or four miles to the gaol. We had no motor transport to shift all the heavy gear, but we used the bare chassis of old motor vehicles as trailers. We would pile these trailers up with building materials and attach a long rope to the front with bits of wood at intervals, as crosspieces. Up to twenty-five men would pull these trailers, straining against the crosspieces of wood like human oxen. Our old huts were set up outside the gaol walls.

I preferred to live outside the gaol, because it was more light and airy in these 100-metre-long *atap* huts. You had your bunk space, and you could see everyone. Inside the gaol it was three men to a cell. They weren't very big – about eight feet long by seven feet wide. There was a big concrete block in the middle of the cell that could be used as a bed by one man, and the other two had to lie down on either side on the floor. We lost a lot of amenities when we moved to the gaol, mainly because there was less space. We couldn't have entertainment like the Changi Theatre because there simply wasn't room for it. The Concert Party did survive though, and finally got permission to set up a small stage in a courtyard within the gaol, and were able to put on limited concerts from time to time with the approval of the Japanese.

Before we moved from Selarang Barracks I was able to spend some time in my little darkroom at the pump-house, which was still undisturbed. I had buried bottles of developer and fixer before I went to the railway, and I had some photographic paper that I had souvenired from the Singapore docks very early on. I even made some contact prints of some of the photos I had taken in Thailand and was foolish enough to give various people some copies. Some of the senior officers got to hear about this and they thought it was like holding on to a bag of dynamite. I was warned on several occasions that if I was caught with a camera I'd be severely dealt with. But they didn't know I had already broken the camera up. I kept them guessing and, as soon as I found out that the official attitude towards my photography was hostile, I kept the photos out of sight. They were hidden away in a variety of places, and sometimes buried.

The biggest problem was what to do with the photos when we were shifting from Selarang Barracks to Changi Gaol. The Japanese had greater access to us and they were searching our belongings more thoroughly. Then again, I had to be sure I didn't lose track of where they were, because a lot of buildings were being demolished. So I retrieved most of the material I had and hid it in an area just outside the walls of the gaol, but within the compound I was living in. I had little spots in the huts which were framed with bamboo. I would cut an opening in a hollow bamboo section like a little door. Then I would wrap the photographs and negatives in a piece of cloth, and store them in the hollow exterior of the bamboo. There were plenty of rubber trees about and I would use some of the latex to glue the little door I had cut out of the bamboo back into place so it wouldn't be noticed.

One day early in 1945, Black Jack Galleghan called me in and said: 'Aspinall, I've got to get you back home and I won't take any short cuts to do it. If you've got contraband material, we'll get it from you. If you're caught with it, don't expect any sympathy from me.'

I said: 'Well, I've got photographic material, Sir. It's hidden away and it will stay that way until such time as we look like going home.'

Black Jack said: 'Well, I'll tell you something. We have a special container that is going to be buried shortly with a lot of secret and sensitive records we want preserved. I want you to give me that photographic material and we will include it in the container to be buried.'

I had no hesitation in handing my negatives and prints over, and I understand that the container was buried down one of the latrine bore-holes, ready to be recovered after the war.

Although I had stopped dabbling with photography, I still had plenty to do. I became involved with some of the secret radio work that brought us news from the outside world, news that was getting better and better from the Allied point of view. Now I'd developed the reputation of being a bit of a scrounger, and I got interested in helping with the manufacture of artificial limbs to help the poor blokes who had lost legs in battle, or following amputations on the railway. I didn't take part in the actual construction of the artificial limbs, but the man who was making the limbs, Arthur Purdon, would ask me if I could get him little springs or bolts, or bits of aluminium or duralumin from crashed Japanese aircraft in the vicinity of the Changi aerodrome – which we were helping to extend at the time.

Just about every second POW was a scrounger by fair means or foul. We regarded the Japanese as fair game. If we could pinch something from them, we would. The native population had much the same idea, and a lot of the material we scrounged would be sold to the Chinese for food – the Japanese money wasn't worth anything. Petrol was a good commodity. A couple of gallons of petrol was worth about a dozen coconuts or a hand of bananas. We developed quite a complex trading system with the Asian community and it was very successful. Our prime needs were food, medicines or drugs if possible, and they needed materials of any description to help in their businesses. We had a very good relationship with the local people.

A friend and I used to go out at night from Changi Gaol to get the bits and pieces from crashed Japanese aircraft, mainly on behalf of the artificial limb factory. But one particular night when we were getting some of this stuff, my mate said to me, 'Gee I'd like to get down among some of the operational Jap planes and set them on fire.'

I said, 'Oh you might do one or two, but you'd have the whole Jap army on your back before very long.' But the idea stayed in our minds, and we decided to go down to the operational aircraft area one night to see what was happening down there. The Japanese Air Force had taken over the whole Changi aerodrome complex, and we knew they were using the old Roberts Barracks as a store and housing for their personnel. Anyway, one dark night we did go down to the Roberts Barracks area, and we poked around the various buildings. In one we found a lot of Japanese radial aircraft engines. They were sitting on stands, obviously being dismantled and serviced. Some of them had their cylinder heads off and we thought we might have a chance of sabotaging some of the engines. The place was pretty lightly guarded. A lot of the Chinese used to wander about at night, and the Jap guards were rather slack. You could hear them walking up and down the rows of aircraft and talking, but they seemed to be enjoying themselves rather than guarding the aircraft. We would move along a deep monsoon drain near the particular building we wanted to explore, making sure it was a moonless night. After a few visits we got to know where the guards were likely to be. If we were ever spotted, we had a plan to split up and run in different directions, to get back to camp.

My mate and I kept the idea of sabotage in mind while we explored around the Changi aerodrome on various night excursions. One night, we were over in the Selarang Barracks area near a transport garage by the old Changi Theatre. The Japs were using it as a mechanical workshop for trucks and other vehicles and we noticed a stack of batteries in one corner beside a big battery charger and lots of wicker-covered glass jars. We had a suspicion these jars might have battery acid – sulphuric acid – in them, so we brought one back to Changi Gaol to test it. When we poured some on to a piece of tin, it ate its way straight through, so it must have been undiluted sulphuric acid. We got hold of some old pickle jars, and half-filled them with the sulphuric acid and made a holder plaited out of coconut leaves, as it was very dangerous stuff to handle. I had a brief discussion with one of our senior officers about what we had in mind, and he seemed to be quite happy about it. We made up a couple of brushes out of pieces of bamboo with the ends roughed and teased out, and set off one night to see what we could do to the aircraft engines to put them out of action.

Once inside the workshop, we felt our way to the work benches, and groped around until we found the ones with the cylinder heads off. Because they were radial engines, we couldn't pour anything into the bottom cylinders, because it would have just run out. We opened up our pickle jars of acid, and carefully brushed it inside the five or so cylinders that were on top of the engine. We managed to do about eight engines, before making our way back to Changi Gaol as quickly as we could.

We didn't know for sure what the results of our work would be, but when we saw what the acid did to a piece of tin, we thought it would cause some kind of corrosion to the cylinders of the aero engines. By this time the Americans were sending B29 bombers over Singapore, and the Japanese would scramble their Zero fighters to go after them. I do know that on several occasions – after we had done our job with the acid – several of the fighters returned very quickly after taking off. Some of them didn't make the aerodrome, and flew straight into the coconut trees at the end of the runway.

TO ALL ALLIED PRISONERS OF WAR

THE JAPANESE FORCES HAVE SURRENDERED UNCONDITIONALLY AND THE WAR IS OVER

WE will get supplies to you as soon as is humanly possible and will make arrangements to get you out but, owing to the distances involved, it may be some time before we can achieve this.

YOU will help us and yourselves if you act as follows :—

(1) Stay in your camp until you get further orders from us.

(2) Start preparing nominal rolls of personnel giving fullest particulars.

(3) List your most urgent necessities.

(4) If you have been starved or underfed for long periods DO NOT eat large quantities of solid food, fruit or vegetables at first. It is dangerous for you to do so. Small quantities at frequent intervals are much safer and will strengthen you far more quickly. For those who are really ill or very weak, fluids such as broth and soup, making use of the water in which rice and other foods have been boiled, are much the best. Gifts of food from the local population should be cooked. We want to get you back home quickly, safe and sound, and we do not want to risk your chances from diarrhoea, dysentry and cholera at this last stage.

(5) Local authorities and/or Allied officers will take charge of your affairs in a very short time. Be guided by their advice.

Copies of this leaflet were dropped over Changi on 28 August 1945. The reverse side contained instructions to the Japanese about the treatment of prisoners. The annotation on the left of the leaflet has been made by the diarist of the 8th Australian Division. (AWM no. 128460)

It isn't possible to say that this had anything to do with our sabotage effort, but the engines were making spluttering noises when the planes came down and we thought – and hoped – it might have been the result of our work on that dark night.

That was the last time we went near the aero workshops. Several weeks later, we met one of our Chinese contacts, who said there had been some kind of investigation by Japanese engineers. He said that the radial engines had had all their cylinder sleeves replaced, and some bad things had been happening. When I asked what had been going on, he said: 'Oh the Japanese rounded up a lot of Asian workers down there, and they made them stand in line for two days while they were interrogated. I think it is something to do with the aeroplane engines.'

A little later he told me that four or five of the Asians were taken down to Changi Beach and shot. Now I never did know whether it was a result of our sabotage attempts, but I have often felt very upset that possibly other people had been punished for our actions. In fact, after finding out as much as I could about what had happened down at Roberts Barracks, I spoke to the senior officer I had previously briefed on our sabotage plans. I told him that it was possible that, as a result of what we had done, the Japanese had blamed some Asian workers and a number of them had been shot. I was very quickly told to cease any further action against the Japanese in that way, that there was to be no more sabotage, and no more going outside the gaol perimeter. In other words, I was to stay put and behave myself. It was explained to me that the Japanese always took severe reprisals on anyone they felt might be connected with sabotage, as a deterrent. We knew that the war was almost over, and it would be silly to have large numbers of Australian prisoners of war shot at such a late stage, after having survived so much. I did as I was told.

The final months in Changi were very difficult. There was very little food and I think this was the same for the Japanese and the local population as well. We were getting very weak, and there were well-sourced rumours that the Japanese planned to machine-gun us into freshly dug trenches outside the gaol in the event of an Allied landing. Some weeks before the war did end, we heard references on our secret radios to the effect that the end of the war was in sight. We could never understand this, but one particular night I was listening to a BBC news broadcast from Delhi and the news came through that an atom bomb had been dropped on Japan. Now we had no idea what an atom bomb was. Well, the following night I was operating a radio again and we heard the news that a second atom bomb had been dropped on Japan. By this time we had more of an idea what an atom bomb was, but it was something beyond my imagination. All I knew was that it was a different type of bomb that burned up literally everything within miles of it when it was dropped. I think we knew about what was happening in Japan before the Japanese who controlled us did. But there was a slight alteration in their attitude.

Then all work outside the gaol stopped and most of the Japanese guards just disappeared, leaving only a small number in charge of us. We heard that the war had ended and the Japanese Emperor had announced the unconditional surrender of the Japanese forces. But the Japanese at Changi didn't know this for some time, and it wasn't until some Allied aircraft flew overhead and dropped a lot of leaflets that they realised that the war was over. At that point we produced one of our radios and set it up on one of the gaol walls and turned it up, and thousands of prisoners of war stood listening to it. The broadcast described the events of the last week or so and actually included a speech from the Japanese Emperor about Japan's unconditional surrender. There were instructions for all Japanese troops to withdraw into groups, and that prisoners of war were to take over their own areas. They were to remain where they were until they heard from their own people. And that's how we became free again, in August 1945.

There were some reprisals. I understand some of our military police rounded up quite a number of the extremely bad Japanese and it was said some of them offered resistance. Shotguns were obtained from somewhere and a number of Japanese were found shot down on Changi Beach. Whether they were shot by our people, or by the Chinese, I don't know. But this kind of thing was exceptional. Most of us were so pleased and elated that it was over, and we'd be going back home, we weren't looking for revenge. In fact nearly all of us were so weak and skinny and low in health that it was an achievement just to get up and walk from point A to point B, let alone trying to kill or beat up Japanese or Korean guards. I have no doubt that some of this went on and perhaps if we had been in better health and condition it might have been a different story. But it was food, not revenge, that was uppermost in our minds. Most of us were walking skeletons, and we were looking forward to better things to come.

The first Allied troops to arrive at Changi Gaol were some British and Indian soldiers. We didn't see any Australians for the first few days, until two Mosquito fighter planes landed on the Changi aerodrome we had helped to build. The pilots said they would fly low over the gaol when they left, and they certainly did. There was a big clock tower over the front gate, and the two planes seemed to be heading straight for it. Then just at the last moment, one went to the left, and one went to the right. It looked as though they were going to crash.

When we took over control of our own affairs again, Black Jack Galleghan moved into a palatial house outside the gaol. He sent for me and said he needed a stove. I went down to a Japanese camp nearby and helped myself to a Ford Prefect car and took a few of my friends with me to see if we could find Black Jack a stove. After some poking about, we found one in some Japanese officers' quarters. It was a beauty, a General Electric with four burners and an oven. The trouble was, it wouldn't fit through the door of the Ford Prefect. I left one of our chaps to look after the Prefect – I wasn't going to lose sight of that – and managed to acquire a small truck. We loaded the stove on, with a couple of blokes riding on the tray to hold it.

After we connected up Black Jack's stove, we shot into Singapore in the Prefect. A Royal Australian Navy corvette had just pulled in to the dock area and we went on board and had the greatest feed of our lives. So much so that we got quite ill. The leaflets that were lying around everywhere were warning us not to eat too much, and just have light soups and fruit, and that kind of thing. We thought that was a big joke. But I couldn't eat more than half a plate of the meat stew the navy gave us. I pushed my plate to one side and got stuck into a tin of peaches, with some tinned cream. We just gorged ourselves. I must have been a bit weak in the stomach, because I had a tummy ache all the next day.

I started a kind of ferry service between Singapore and Changi Gaol, using my little Ford Prefect. One day I met some New Zealand padres and some women reporters who were looking for the prisoners of war. One padre had a box of fifty pipes, and cakes of tobacco. I took delivery of them and drove them back to Changi.

We sort of went wild for the week before the Australian rescue personnel came in and set up provosts around the gaol perimeter. We weren't supposed to leave the area without a good excuse. But Black Jack gave me a pass, a very official-looking document with a scrawled signature. I used that to get into Singapore whenever I wanted to.

Petrol was no problem. There was a Jap guard house down the road and every time I drove past the half a dozen Japs there, they would jump up and salute. I noticed some petrol drums in the yard. I asked them if the drums contained gasoline, and they very politely said 'yes'. There were five or six 44-gallon drums of petrol, a hand pump and some jerry cans. The Japs used to help me pump the petrol out of the drums.

After about two weeks of this kind of life, we heard we were to embark on a ship called the *Esperance Bay*. She had been one of the Bay Line passenger ships before the war, and was now a troop transport.

I managed to drive down to the docks in some style in my trusty Ford Prefect, acting as driver for the CO of the 2/29th Battalion, Colonel SAF Pond. I parked the Prefect in a shed near the *Esperance Bay* and took the rotor out of the distributor on board with me. I had a sneaking feeling I might get a chance to use the car again.

When we got on board, we were issued with new khaki drill clothes, but the ship didn't sail that night. A friend of mine, Sergeant Len Barnes, and I took off in the Prefect and drove ourselves into Singapore again. We met up with some Australian troops in a big, open-air restaurant, and didn't get back to the ship until 2 am the next day. I put the Prefect back in the shed, but that was the last trip I did in her.

We sailed the next morning at 10 am – 23 September 1945 – bound for Australia. We all stood along the rail and had a last look at Singapore Island disappearing behind us. Some of us were muttering things like:

'Goodbye you land of stinking smells and sorrow

An inch of rain today and none tomorrow.'

Most just stood in silence at the stern as Singapore faded from view. We had very mixed thoughts, but they were mostly of our future, home, and who we were going to see there. Not many of us slept that night; we just wandered about the ship. The *Esperance Bay* was ablaze with lights. We were steaming in a convoy and a darkened navy escort kept darting about and circling us, possibly checking for mines. It was just like a dream. A great feeling.

We arrived off Darwin at night, and the next morning we could see the port was in a bit of a mess due to the Japanese bombing raids during the war. The *Esperance Bay* anchored about half a mile off shore, and at 10 am a group of launches came out to take us ashore.

It was just tremendous to see so many familiar-looking Australian faces. There was a crowd waiting at the docks, a great lovely sea of Australian faces yelling and cheering. Some of the blokes kissed the ground as they stepped ashore. By gee I can tell you I wouldn't have been ashamed to have done it!

Various activities had been organised for us and I went with a group to the RAAF base just outside Darwin. We had lunch there and looked over the base and inspected aircraft like the Liberator bombers which we hadn't seen close-up before. When we got back to the wharf, there were a couple of Catalina flying boats there and an RAAF officer asked if any of us would like a ride. Ten or fifteen of us crowded on to each Catalina and off we went for a joyride around Darwin. We had three attempts to take off, as we were overloaded. When we landed, we hit the water so hard I thought we had crashed.

Back on board the *Esperance Bay*, we were issued with our winter serge uniforms. They were handed out whether they fitted or not, but by swapping with our mates, we finished up with a reasonable fit. We were paraded on deck with our new uniforms – but no rifles. We had finished with them.

We sailed down the east coast of Australia quite close to land. I remember seeing the Byron Bay lighthouse. Some of the chaps who lived in that area said they might as well jump off and swim home.

As in Darwin, we arrived in Sydney at night, and stood off Clifton Gardens until daylight. A great collection of launches and small boats came out waving placards of welcome, and signs with different names on them, calling out for soldiers they knew. Finally about 9 am the *Esperance Bay* berthed at No 11 wharf Woolloomooloo, but we had to stay on board for a few more hours. Then we were taken through the city in double-decker buses, with people yelling and cheering and shouting. The city seemed to come to a standstill. Our destination was Ingleburn Army Camp, where we were to meet our relatives.

You had to wait till your name was called out and then you walked down the side of a little grassy hill. I was reunited with my mother and other members of my family. It was one big, happy reunion.

A few weeks later I received word from our CO, now Brigadier Galleghan, that he had my photographs in his possession – they had been recovered from the canister buried in the Changi bore-hole – and would I like to come and talk to him about them. I went to his Mosman home and he picked out various negatives and prints he wanted to use as evidence at the Rabaul war crimes trials.

The Rabaul war crimes trials took place towards the end of 1946, and I presume the material I gave Brigadier Galleghan had been set up for the court to view by the Intelligence section of the Australian Army. I was told that it was set up in some kind of display. Apparently a photographer from the Melbourne *Argus* managed to rephotograph a lot of my work, because many of my photos were published in that paper later on, as well as other material on display there. I even found out much later that some of my photos had been printed up into a numbered set and were on sale in Melbourne, and advertised in some magazines for a certain price. I'm not sure of the full details, but I was very angry and upset at the time that someone was making money out of my photos in a way that was never intended.

In fact Black Jack Galleghan had spoken to me about the publication of my photos when I was approached by a newspaper man as we were waiting to disembark from the ship that brought us from Singapore. He pointed out that there were a lot of people in my photos who hadn't come back, and that publication would be painful for their families and loved ones. So I put them away and virtually forgot about them for many years. But as time has passed, I think it's all part of our history, and that is one reason why I am happy to see them displayed and published in this book. Unfortunately some of my material never did return from the Rabaul war crimes trials. I did speak to Brigadier Galleghan about it before he died, but he was unable to say what had happened to the missing photos.

I sometimes wonder whether the experiences I had as a prisoner of war of the Japanese changed my character at all. It's difficult to tell. I find I tend to get irritable at times, but I try to keep a hold on myself and keep occupied with various projects. I've kept up an interest in photography, particularly 16-mm movie work. I certainly don't brood about the bad things that happened, and I quite like talking about some of the brighter side of our POW life. Not that I talk about it much at all, really. But I think I probably understand people's problems better now, having been a prisoner of war – particularly people with social problems, or who are under extreme stress.

My own health is not all that good. I've lost the sight of one eye and my second eye is deteriorating all the time and has been doing so for many years. It's probably concerned with malnutrition and vitamin deficiencies while I was a prisoner of war.

My attitudes to the Japanese have not changed since the war. I will never forget a conversation I had once with a Japanese officer on the Thai–Burma Railway. He said to me one day, 'How long you think war last?'

I said, 'Maybe another year, maybe another couple of years.'

'Oh,' he said, 'it will be all over by then. Japan will have Australia . . . Japan will have all countries in this part of the world.'

I asked him what would happen if Japan didn't get those countries?

'Ah,' he said, 'even if it takes one hundred years, Japan will own Australia.'

I've always had that in the back of my mind, that given a similar opportunity – they'd do it all again. I don't think they've changed all that much.

SOURCES

ALL THE DIRECT QUOTES IN 'THE POW EXPERIENCE' (UNLESS OTHERWISE SPECIFIED) ARE TAKEN from the original oral history tapes used in the broadcast documentary series *Prisoners Of War: Australians under Nippon* first broadcast by the Australian Broadcasting Corporation in 1984.

Quotes on the reception of Dunlop Force at Changi taken from *Arthur Blackburn, VC: an Australian hero, his men and their two World Wars*, by Andrew Faulkner, Wakefield Press, 2008, and gratefully acknowledged.

Reference books include:

Prisoners Of War: Australians Under Nippon, Hank Nelson, ABC Books, 1985

Prisoners Of The Japanese, A J Sweeting, Part III of *The Japanese Thrust: Australia In The War of 1939–45*, Lionel Wigmore, The Griffin Press, 1957

Behind Bamboo, Rohan D Rivett, Angus & Robertson, 1947

One Man's War, Stan Arneil, Alternative Publishing Co-Operative, 1980

Kill the Prisoners, Don Wall, published by D Wall, 1997

INDEX

Page numbers in *italics* refer to picture captions